D0001939

# COLLECTING
# **BOOKS**

# COLLECTING
# **BOOKS**

Matthew Budman

**HOUSE OF COLLECTIBLES**

NEW YORK

THIS BOOK IS THE PROPERTY OF
THE NATIONAL CITY PUBLIC LIBRARY
1401 NATIONAL CITY BLVD
NATIONAL CITY, CA 91950

Instant Expert: Collecting Books

by Matthew Budman

Copyright © 2004 by Random House, Inc.

Important Notice: All the information, including valuations, in this book has been compiled from reliable sources, and efforts have been made to eliminate errors and questionable data. Nevertheless, the possibility of error, in a work of such immense scope, always exists. The publisher will not be responsible for any losses that may occur in the purchase, sale, or other transaction of items because of information contained herein. Readers who feel they have discovered errors are invited to write and inform us, so they may be corrected in subsequent editions.

All rights reserved under International and Pan-American Copyright Conventions. Published in the United States by House of Collectibles, a member of The Random House Information Group, a division of Random House, Inc., New York and simultaneously in Canada by Random House of Canada Limited, Toronto. No part of this book may be reproduced in any form or by any means, electronic or mechanical, including photocopying, recording, or by any information storage and retrieval system, without the written permission of the publisher. All inquiries should be addressed to House of Collectibles, Random House Information Group, 1745 Broadway, New York, NY 10019.

House of Collectibles and colophon are registered trademarks of Random House, Inc.

RANDOM HOUSE is a registered trademark of Random House, Inc.

This book is available for special discounts for bulk purchases for sales promotions or premiums. Special editions, including personalized covers, excerpts of existing books, and corporate imprints, can be created in large quantities for special needs. For more information, write to Special Markets/Premium Sales, 1745 Broadway, MD 6-2, New York, NY 10019 or e-mail specialmarkets@randomhouse.com.

Please address inquiries about electronic licensing of reference products for use on a network, in software or on CD-ROM to the Subsidiary Rights Department, Random House Reference, fax 212-572-6003.

Visit the Random House Web site: www.randomhouse.com.

Library of Congress Cataloging-in-Publication Data is available.

First Edition

0 9 8 7 6 5 4 3 2 1

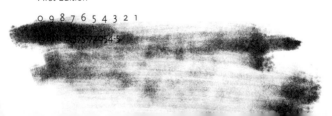

# CONTENTS

# ACKNOWLEDGMENTS

For teaching me to read at a ridiculously early age: my mother, Sheila, and grandmother, Edie.

For instilling invaluable bargain-hunting instincts: both my parents.

For helping to carry all those crates: Brian Ilfeld; my father, Ken; and the guys from Bekins Moving Services and Able Metro Moving & Storage. Special thanks to Brian for agreeing to begin speaking to me again.

For designing and manufacturing the shelves that dominate our house: Ikea.

For filling those shelves: Advanced Book Exchange, eBay, and bookstores and friends-of-the-library organizations on both coasts.

For inside information: Ken Eastman at Moe's Books, Carey G. Spain at Montclair Book Center, Eugene Okamoto at Harvest Book Co., Ken Gloss at Brattle Book Shop, Joel Dumas at North Country Books, and especially Phil Arundel at Arundel Books.

For making this book happen: Jay Stevenson, Ph.D., for showing me the possibilities; Will Weisser, for opening the door at Crown; Jim Walsh, for helping me through it;

eagle-eyed Bob Riedel, for catching several potentially embarrassing omissions and inclusions; and Dorothy Harris and Lindsey Glass at House of Collectibles, for offering their confidence, support, and enthusiasm.

For advice, input, and encouragement: Jen Dussling, Stephanie Volmer, Nicholas Latimer, Jonathan McFall, Jennifer Freer, and Regina Feeney.

For ongoing stimulation and feedback, not to mention eleventh-hour editing more thorough and incisive than either expected or warranted: Vic Tulli.

And for agreeing to spend a lifetime surrounded by, and occasionally overwhelmed by, stacks and shelves and teetering piles of books: my muse, Cristina Beltrán.

# INTRODUCTION

Maybe you find yourself surrounded by books and aren't sure whether it all constitutes a genuine collection. Maybe you suspect that some of your books are worth a lot more than you paid for them—or that they're not as valuable as you'd hoped. Maybe, simply, you're fascinated by the book-collecting hobby and don't know where to begin.

Whatever the reasons that drew you to pick up this small volume, it can help.

"Have you *read* all these?" is invariably the first thing people ask when they see all the shelves. Silly question—don't they understand what collecting is all about? Some books you own because you intend to read them; some you own *just to have.*

(Not to mention that it's impossible to have made it through all these books at my age—or at *any* age.)

Here's one definition of when you make the move from reader to collector: *as soon as you buy a book that you have no intention of reading.* Perhaps you've read, or will read, a different copy of the same title—but not this one. Why would you want a book you plan never to open? Well . . .

Perhaps it's a rare first edition of a favorite novel.

Maybe you've decided to accumulate books in its genre.

Because it once belonged to someone famous.

Or maybe it's just a lovely old volume that gives you a warm feeling to hold.

You don't need a reason, really. This is what collecting books is all about. You can devote hours to research and purchase a single carefully selected volume each month; you can snatch up armloads at library sales; you can spend each Saturday cruising yard sales. You can have a roomful—or a houseful—of meticulously organized books in climate-controlled cases, or a single shelf of prizes. It all qualifies. The principles are the same no matter what your level of commitment.

Welcome to the world's greatest hobby.

## You Can't Buy Everything

Historically speaking, you're catching the bug at a great time. This is a hobby that has thrived since books were invented more than two millennia ago, and in recent years it has become increasingly democratic, open to people of every interest and background and level of disposable income, thanks largely to the Internet.

Where do you fit in? Wherever you want; wherever you can. It's not a contest.

You'll find out soon enough: There are people out there with far more resources and space than you have, people who can drop hundreds or thousands of dollars on an item they want without a second thought. You can't compete head-to-head, so don't try—have fun playing the game, and feel free to change the rules.

And don't envy the rich folks too much: The hunt is much of what's fun about the hobby, and they're missing it. In an April 2000 *Gentlemen's Quarterly* feature, author Owen Edwards advised the novice collector looking to spend $20,000 on rare books to simply visit a high-end antiquarian bookshop and leave with three or four precious volumes in hand. A quick and effortless haul, to be sure, but utterly impersonal, unchallenging, and even boring.

As John Carter writes in the classic *Taste and Technique in Book Collecting*, "It is a very easy matter nowadays to find a *First Folio* or a first edition of Johnson's *Dictionary* and a man needs neither imagination nor persistence to possess himself of a copy of either: all he needs is a cheque-book."

Well, I'm assuming that if you intend to drop $20,000 on books, you'll take more than an hour to do it, and that you'll end up with enough to fill at least a few shelves, along with a story to go with each volume—a story of, perhaps, imagination and persistence. Without those stories, what's the point?

## It's All About the Book

Even though collecting is all about taking books *out* of circulation—of subverting their intended purpose—the hobby begins, of course, with reading. America may be a nation of TV junkies, but millions of us splurge on the new Stephen Ambrose war history, cruise the New Additions tray at the local public library, debate whether the new Don DeLillo novel lives up to the hype, hope that this week's financial guru is offering sound investment advice, pick up a James Patterson paperback at the airport, or plunk down $25 to have our political convictions reinforced or refuted.

We join reading groups in massive numbers. For city-wide let's-all-read-one-book programs, politicians debate which novel (*To Kill a Mockingbird? Native Speaker? A Lesson Before Dying?*) is most appropriate for residents to buy en masse. Inspired by Oprah Winfrey's success, TV shows and bookstores have raced to create book clubs.

Perhaps someday we'll all get pleasure and information exclusively from little LCD screens, but for now the book itself—in the same recognizable form for the last five centuries—continues to thrive as a means of entertainment, of communication, of persuasion, of incitement. And all this is great news for collectors: Millions of readers put millions of used books into circulation every year, ready to go back out into the world.

Now, there are few book collectors who aren't avid readers as well. But there's a difference between them—us—and people who take out library books or highlight passages in self-help memoirs or buy that *New York Times* best-seller because all their friends have recommended it. Collectors want, need, to *possess* the books—and not just books you love, but the *most desirable* copies of the books you love.

That difference makes all the difference. It's not about just the words on the pages—*it's about the books themselves*.

## On Your Mark . . . Get Set . . .

What do you want from your books? If you're buying purely for investment—to amass a collection to be stored in a vault for your children to sell after you die—that's one thing. That type of collector should approach books as he would stocks, real estate, or paintings: with research, a trusted dealer, and a long-range plan.

I'm assuming that you want something different: to begin building a library whose sole purpose is to give you pleasure, in the hunt as well as the prizes.

Realizing that should be a liberation: There are no boundaries.

It doesn't even matter if the books in which you're interested aren't all that valuable. You can think of the fact that the vast majority of poetry books or romantic novels or autographed political memoirs are not considered collectible as an *opportunity*.

Again, the object of collecting should be to surround yourself with books that make you happy—and proud. If they happen to be worth a lot, that's a bonus.

This doesn't mean, of course, that getting ripped off is OK. It's not—which is why, later in the book, I'll talk about why those John Grisham first editions aren't such a great investment, how to make sure that the book you're paying for is the one you get, and how there's money to be made selling books—but that making that money may drain the hobby of the fun that you got into it for.

You'll also learn things about the hobby that have nothing to do with monetary value: why bookstores offer buying opportunities and experiences that the Internet can't duplicate, places to find used books that you may not even know about, why different copies of the same title can look nothing alike, the supreme importance of condition, the best ways to sell or donate the books you don't want in order to make room for the books you do, and the trickiest bit of all—how to tell if a book is a first edition.

All in all, I hope, enough to get you started.

So: You're at a bookstore, or cruising eBay, or at a library sale, and a colorful dust jacket catches your eye. Now what?

# 1

## WHAT YOU NEED TO KNOW TO START

### "What Do You Collect?"

Where to begin, if not a stuffy, overpriced, glass-encased store? Start with what you like.

Visit a local used bookstore and browse the racks; think of subjects that have always caught your attention; look at books you already own; recall favorite travel sagas or guilty-pleasure novels; explore intriguing oddities. John T. Winterich writes in *A Primer of Book Collecting*: "Whatever a man's hobby, he can parallel it—or his trade, his profession, even his pet aversion—in book collecting."

Love your job? Seek out books that champion the profession or explore its history.

Hate your job? Try books that attack it. (And keep the library door shut when you invite your boss over.)

In *Among the Gently Mad*, Nicholas Basbanes advises bibliophiles to think of themselves as storytellers and each collection as "a form of narrative," with a plot line that is "as much a reflection of personality and purpose as it is of life experience."

As you spend time with and among different titles and categories, you'll happen upon a collecting focus; it'll appear organically. And in the process of researching, sifting, and beginning your collection, you'll become an authority on your particular subject. You'll learn about how these books fit into the culture at large, about tastes of the time, about why particular books had disproportionately great impact—or no impact at all.

Perhaps most appealing: You'll find yourself part of a community interested in the same general area; you'll run into the same people at the same tables at book sales and the same aisles at bookstores, and bidding on the same eBay auctions.

If you think your choice of focus is overly insular or idiosyncratic or, well, kooky, I assure you it's not: Ask around and you'll find people who collect just about everything. Here are some focuses that I've seen or read about or that just *seem* as though they'd be great subjects for people to collect:

Novels set in Florida

Atomic-age books about how to survive a nuclear war

Pulitzer Prize–winning biographies

Vintage diet books

Books with cover art by Edward Gorey

Nineteenth-century volumes warning about the dangers of dancing

Books about railroads

Contemporaneous accounts of World War I

Reportage about natural disasters

Books about short-lived fads, from hula hoops to Pac-Man

Photoplay editions of westerns

Memoirs of residents of Ohio

Mystery novels that take place aboard trains

Books whose titles derive from Shakespearean quotes

Civil War–era fiction

Collections of cartoons about business

Hollywood exposés published during the silent era

Volumes of reproductions of Cubist paintings

Books about Watergate—not just the best-sellers but the more obscure titles

A few other possibilities:

- Pick several favorite authors and try to compile a comprehensive library of their works—every edition, every translation, every iteration. Hardcovers, paperbacks, advance copies, reprints.

- Find a favorite series—for instance, the City Lights Pocket Poets collection or Carolyn Keene's Nancy Drew stories—and start tracking down each volume, the best copy you can find of each. Some will be easy and cheap, others far more elusive.

- Start collecting first editions of the No. 1 best-seller—fiction and nonfiction—of each year of the twentieth century. Some are obscure, some completely forgotten, and some still in print.

No matter what you decide to zoom in on, as soon as you begin searching hard, you'll find much more than you anticipated. And the narrower your focus, the better the chance of having one of the best—perhaps even *the* best—collections of that particular focus in existence.

Besides, you can't collect everything. An aspiring collector, wrote J. Herbert Slater in his 1905 *How to Collect Books*, *must* narrow his focus: "[B]ooks are so numerous, and many of them so difficult to acquire that he must have something of the specialist about him if he would be a collector in the modern acceptation of the term."

## The Human Factor

Of course, just because you've picked a specialty doesn't mean you should simply ignore titles outside it—otherwise you'd whip through every book sale and shop in a matter of minutes. There's a world of books out there, and some of them belong in your possession. And so you'll find yourself picking up an unfamiliar book and facing the most basic question: *Is this worth buying?*

Helping you answer that question is, in large part, what this book is about.

How do you determine whether a book has value? Well, it'd be nice if there were simple collectibility rules that anyone could memorize, if you didn't *need* a book to offer guidance, if you could pick up a book and look for a mark that would clearly indicate whether you should tuck it under your arm or return it to the shelf.

Nice, sure . . . but not much fun, or challenge, or mystery, or magic.

The enormous variety and variability of books are part of what makes this an exciting hobby. Any given volume may differ from one adjacent to it by any number of factors: age, author, title, prior owner, publisher, edition, condition. There are always questions and uncertainty and *humanness*, and that's what keeps book collecting from becoming just a business.

The human factor is apparent in the hunt as well as the books themselves. Whether you're bidding against an eBay buyer on the other side of the country or scouring the same library-sale table as another browser with the same "want list," collecting carries an element of competition. A book must be desirable to carry any value, meaning that demand must outstrip supply—more people want it than can own it.

You can think of it as a game—if you want to, that is. Either way, when a prized item is safely in your possession, at a price that makes you grin, you've won. The converse is that collecting is not a war: You can't attend every book sale and frequent every bookstore in the country, or even monitor what every online seller makes available every minute of every day, so stop thinking about all that you might be missing. Just go for what you want and reasonably can get, and don't worry about the rest.

## Launched into the World

In picking up a volume that looks intriguing—or one that you already own but know nothing about—you'll find yourself running over a standard series of questions: Who's the author? What's the title? subject area? publisher? condition? year of publication? Are you familiar with the book, or baffled by it? And a key question: Is it a first edition?

First things first: What is a first edition, anyway? All too often, non-collectors use the term to describe an old book, a book that *looks* valuable, or any hardcover volume at all, but it means something very specific.

Strictly, a first edition is the first *form* of a book, before it's revised or reset in a new format or font. A book may go into multiple printings but may still be considered a first edition. That's only technically, though. When you say *first edition*, what you mean is *first edition, first printing*—the first print run of the first regular form of a book.

Many times, the only distinction between a first printing and a second printing is the absence or presence of a tiny "1" on the copyright page—and that tiny "1" can make a huge difference in value: A later printing of a modern novel is typically worth a fraction of a first.

What's so special about first editions? A first represents the launching of a work into the world, with or without fanfare, to have a great impact, or no impact, immediately or decades later. Some all-time classics (*Moby-Dick*, *Walden*) sold only a handful of copies the first time they hit bookstore shelves—if they hit them at all. Others were instant successes. Holding a first edition puts you directly in contact with that moment of impact. "To handle a first edition of Darwin's *Origin of Species* or Newton's *Principia Mathematica*," writes Nicholas Basbanes in *A Gentle Madness*, "is to touch ideas that changed the way people live."

According to bookseller Ken Lopez, firsts originally were highly prized for another reason: Printing presses' metal plates would wear down with repeated pressings, meaning that the first edition's text was actually sharper.

Firsts are all-important to collectors, but it's important to recognize that *every* book has a first edition—most aren't successful enough to warrant reprinting—and that, therefore, the fact of a book being a first is no guarantee of its value. A classic anecdote, from the 1920s: Theater critic Alexander Woollcott was asked to sign a first-edition copy of his book *Shouts and Murmurs*. "Ah, what is so rare as a Woollcott first edition?" he sighed as he scribbled. His compatriot Franklin Pierce Adams quipped: "A Woollcott *second* edition." (Incidentally, if you want a signed first of *Shouts and Murmurs*, it'll cost you well over $200.)

The number of copies in the first printing is determined by the publisher's estimate of how many copies it's likely to sell. Guessing either high or low costs the publisher money: Extra, unsold copies are wasted money, and trips back to the printer are more expensive per copy than if enough had been printed the first time around.

### How to Identify a First

In collecting, what you need to learn how to do, quickly and efficiently, is be able to pick up a book and determine whether it's a first. This is unfortunately—and unnecessarily—complicated by the fact that each publisher elected, years ago, to handle its copyright pages differently. Many don't state *first edition* outright, and a few state it but don't mean it. Some publishers, having established one confusing pattern, have switched several times over the decades—often to even more confusing patterns.

It's a cliché to say, "It's simpler than it sounds," and in this case it would be untrue as well: Identifying firsts and avoiding book-club editions are every bit as complicated as you may have feared. Sure, you can memorize some rules and tips, and by no means should you be discouraged or intimidated, but there's simply too much to remember to cover every book that might catch your eye. *Entire books* exist for only this purpose.

And all this offers another reason to specialize: With any given subject area or author or genre or theme, a relative handful of publishers and patterns will dominate, and you'll quickly learn how to identify them.

Some publishers *do* make it easy, and I won't bother going over those one by one. For these, if you look at the copyright page of a book published after World War II, and it says "First Edition," and it doesn't appear to be a book-club edition, and if there's a string of numbers the lowest of which is 1, then it's probably a first. If only all books were this simple!

Anyway, don't let all this intimidate you. You'll learn pretty quickly, and though there are plenty of exceptions, the basics stay the same.

Beyond what's in these pages, I recommend photocopying the how-to-identify pages from one of the more extensive collecting guidebooks—perhaps Allen and Patricia Ahearn's *Book Collecting*—and carrying them with you on book-hunting excursions, at least until you're comfortable. Bill McBride's pocket guide offers another option. At home, you can tap into the Internet and even more elaborate identification guides.

But this should get you started.

### The First Place to Look

For books published before 1900, it's often as simple as looking at the title page. Is there a year printed there? Then it's probably a first edition. The second place to look is the copyright page. If there's a date listed there—*one* date—and it's the same as the one on the title page, then you can be even more certain.

This is hardly a lock, though—without research, you can never be entirely sure that a nineteenth-century book is a first edition. Whatever the rule, there are any number of exceptions. For instance, if a book was a big seller at the time, it may have been published by several different companies around the same time; one publisher's first edition may appear long after the true first. And many books appeared with a series of slight variations that you'd never notice if you didn't know to look for them—but that make a huge difference to serious collectors. (More on *points* in a bit.)

In the first few decades of the twentieth century, publishers became somewhat better at listing their books' publishing history—but improved little at helping people trying to identify firsts. Most of the time, when you have

The First Place
to Look. No
mystery here
about which
printing this
book is.

COPYRIGHT, 1922, BY
HARCOURT, BRACE AND COMPANY, INC.

Published, September, 1922
Second Printing, October, 1922

to decide quickly, you'll have to rely on evidence that a book is *not* a later printing rather than indications that it *is* a first.

The evidence may be as obvious as a copyright-page statement that a book has been reprinted:

Or it may be more subtle. Some (though not most) publishers put the actual year of a book's publication at the bottom of the title page. If it's later than the date on the copyright page, it's more than likely not a first. (In nineteenth-century books, copyright dates sometimes refer to prior magazine serializations and may precede the first edition's title-page date.)

Therefore, in the absence of easy markers—a "First Printing" statement, a number string, etc.—if the dates are the same, and the copyright page doesn't indicate that the book is a later printing, then it's probably a first.

Now, *since* the 1930s, publishers have settled a bit into some patterns; it isn't *always* a guessing game. Most state on the copyright page something like "First Edition" or "First Printing." In recent years, many have begun using number lines: Both 1 2 3 4 5 6 7 8 9 10 and 1 3 5 7 9 10 8 6 4 2 indicate that a book is a first. With each new printing, publishers remove the lowest number in the sequence, so that number is the key; if it's a 3, then the book is a third printing—*even if it states "First Edition."*

When a publisher neglects to remove that statement for later printings, a quick glance can be misleading.

tional use. For information, please write: Special Collins Publishers, Inc., 10 East 53rd Street, New

FIRST EDITION

*Designed by C. Linda Dingler*

Library of Congress Cataloging-in-Publication Da
Bloom, Amy, 1953–
   Come to me : short stories / Amy Bloom.
     p.  cm.
  ISBN 0-06-018236-9
  I. Title.
PS3552.L6378C65  1993
813'.54—dc20

93 94 95 96 97 ❖/RRD 10 9 8 7 6 5 4 3

**The First Place to Look—A third printing.**
The page says "First Edition," but that 3 in the bottom row indicates that the book was printed later.

Every major publisher does it slightly differently, and it doesn't help that most of them have changed names and policies periodically through the decades. Scribner books can be tough; Harper titles rely on an arcane code of letters. And Random House—the parent publisher of the book you're holding—decided some years ago to add a copyright-page fillip seemingly *only* to confuse people.

Let's look at a few publishers, including those you'll most commonly run across, that *don't* make it all that easy.

**Bantam**
Uses a backward number sequence without an explicit "first" statement: 0 9 8 7 6 5 4 3 2 1.

**Jonathan Cape**
States "First published in Great Britain [year]" or "First published [year]."

**Dutton**
Uses a backward number sequence, usually without an explicit "first" statement: 0 9 8 7 6 5 4 3 2 1. When the publisher remembers to add the statement, it often forgets to take it off for subsequent printings.

**Jonathan Cape.** Look for the "First Published in" line.

First published in Great Britain 1985
Copyright © 1985 by Garp Enterprises, Ltd.

Jonathan Cape Ltd, 32 Bedford Square, London WC1B 3EL

British Library Cataloguing in Publication Data

Irving, John, *1942-*
The Cider House rules.
I. Title
813'.54[F]     PS 3559.R8

ISBN 0-224-02336-5

**Farrar, Rinehart**
**Farrar, Straus**
**Farrar, Straus & Young**

No "first" statement, and no number sequence. The way that Farrar signified firsts was by placing its logo on the copyright page and removing it for subsequent print-ings. In its later incarnations—Farrar, Straus & Cudahy and the longstanding Farrar, Straus & Giroux—the pub-lisher has been much clearer.

**Harcourt**
**Harcourt, Brace**
**Harcourt Brace Jovanovich**

In addition to stating "first edition" or "first American edition," Harcourt uses a string of not numbers but let-ters: A B C D E. This should be easy: If the lowest letter is A, then it's a first printing. But from around 1971 to 1983, the publisher began with B—meaning that a book that looks like a second printing is actually a first, so long as the letters are accompanied by the "first edition" note. (The publisher's first incarnations—Harcourt, Brace and Harcourt, Brace & World—don't use the confusing letter sequence.)

**Harper & Bros.**
**Harper & Row**

Until the 1970s, Harper used a cryptic code of letters (which I won't bother including here) to indicate what year a book was published. In its earliest twentieth-century books, that was the only way to determine if a book was a first; after 1922, the publisher began stating "First Edition." But it sometimes accidentally left the "First" statement on later printings, sending collectors

Copyright © 1973 by John Edgar Wideman
All rights reserved. No part of this publication may
be reproduced or transmitted in any form or by any means,
electronic or mechanical, including photocopy, recording,
or any information storage and retrieval system,
without permission in writing from the publisher.
First edition
ISBN 0-15-154800-5
Library of Congress Catalog Card Number: 72-91841
Printed in the United States of America
B C D E

**Harcourt.** The "B C D E" line normally indicates a second printing, but with this 1973 Harcourt Brace Jovanovich title, it means the book is a first.

back to the letter code. Between 1969 and 1975, Harper further complicated matters by adding a 1-to-10 number row to, unhelpfully, the bottom of the book's last page; after that, the numbers usually appeared on the copyright page. Fortunately, things have settled down over the last three decades, and now identifying a first is pretty clear.

### Houghton Mifflin
Until the late 1950s, Houghton Mifflin didn't signify firsts clearly: It put the date of publication on the title page of first printings and deleted it for later printings. Now the publisher uses a descending number line.

### Alfred A. Knopf
The only tricky element with Knopf's books are those that are reprinted prior to their publication date due to booksellers' orders: These will state "First and second printings before publication" or "First, second, and third printings before publication." They're not considered first editions.

### Macmillan
Beginning in mid-1936—the year it published *Gone With the Wind*—Macmillan began stating "First printing." Before that, the publisher would list the date of each printing; obviously, more than one means that the book isn't a first.

### Random House
The first printing states "First Edition," which is simple enough. But a few decades ago, Random House began adding a number sequence beginning, counterintu-

**Random House.** A first, even though the lowest number is a 2.

I. Title.

PZ4.L965 War 3  [PS3562.U7]  813'.5'4  73-20437
ISBN 0-394-46201-7

Manufactured in the United States of America

2 4 6 8 9 7 5 3

First American Edition

itively, with 2. Most of the time, the "first" statement is removed for later printings, so a second printing states just "24689753."

## Scribner

Between 1930 and the 1970s, the publisher signified a first with an A on the copyright page and changed it to a later letter for subsequent printings. But Scribner couldn't leave well enough alone: Sometimes it added a publisher's seal and/or a code indicating the book's manufacturer and date of publication. Since Scribner published any number of classic novels in the thirties, forties, and fifties, the inconsistencies continue to plague collectors. (To add to the confusion, the name of the publisher itself is unclear—it used to say Charles Scribner's Sons on the title page and Scribners on the spine, and in 1994 the company abbreviated the name to just Scribner.)

## Vanguard

No indication of *anything*. Vanguard sometimes doesn't even bother indicating when a book is a later printing, implying that everything is a first. "Actually," the publisher told researchers Edward Zempel and Linda Verkler in 1976, "there is no way to determine whether our books of the past were first editions or not." Oh well. In the 1970s, some Vanguard books had a number sequence, but that practice didn't last long.

## Viking

In 1937, Viking began stating something like, "First published in [year] by The Viking Press." But a sampling of Viking titles from the last three decades shows some variations (or, uncharitably, carelessness). Some copies have number sequences, some don't. Some state "First American Edition/Published in [year]." Some retain the "First published" line but elsewhere indicate that the book is a later printing. Each case isn't hard to figure out, but the inconsistency is annoying.

## What's the Point of "Points"?

In Raymond Chandler's 1939 classic *The Big Sleep*, detective Philip Marlowe wants to find out whether a bookstore is legitimate, so he drives to the public library and does "a little superficial research in a stuffy volume called Famous First Editions." Then he goes to the bookstore and asks the clerk if she has an 1860 copy of *Ben-Hur*—a third edition, the one "with the erratum on page 116." She tells him no—and thereby fails the detective's test. Why? Because *Ben-Hur* wasn't published until 1880, a fact that any knowledgeable book dealer in 1939 would have known. Marlowe's "erratum" detail is a distraction to make his request sound authentic. It's just the kind of thing a genuine bibliophile would ask about.

The real third printing of Lew Wallace's novel has no erratum on page 116 (though it may in fact have one on page 11). But *Ben-Hur*'s publication history has just the kind of complications that you'd never be able to figure out by looking at its copyright page. The true first's cover is blue-gray, with colored flowers. The author's wife objected to its inappropriate cheeriness, and the publisher, Harper, changed the cover to a plain brown mesh pattern and then to brown pebbled boards. All three of these states are considered first editions, though the only really valuable one is the scarce blue-gray one. But if you want to determine the first printing of the *third* state, there's something else you need to know: After the first printing, to stop concerned readers from asking about the death of his very-much-alive spouse, Wallace altered the book's misleadingly worded dedication from "To the Wife of My Youth" to "To the Wife of My Youth Who Still Abides With Me."

Got it?

The tangled history of *Ben-Hur* isn't all that unusual. For most books, it's enough to follow the rules laid down by their publisher, complex as they are, to identify first edi-

tions. But a surprising number have complex bibliographic histories that require a more careful look or even additional information that you *can't* know without research or guides. (The marks, or elements, that distinguish a first from later editions are known as *points of issue* or just *points*.)

Why so much confusion? A number of reasons.

**What's the Point of "Points"?** The sticker is an immediate tip-off that this copy of *Middlesex* was printed after it won the Pulitzer Prize.

Nineteenth-century books frequently appeared in a number of states, with little to distinguish them. Collectors have spent decades puzzling out which state of certain books came first: the version with one blank page in front, or two? with the typo on page 42, or with the error fixed? With a green dust jacket, or a blue one? Since the earliest state is the most desirable, these clues are of real importance.

Even recent books aren't necessarily easy. Sometimes typographical errors are caught and corrected halfway through a print run, creating a first state and a second state. Or sometimes a book wins an award or gets a great review while the first printing is still on store shelves, and the publisher decides to print new dust jackets and replace the first set.

A sticker or newspaper-review blurb—as opposed to one from *Publishers Weekly* or *Kirkus Reviews*, which appear prior to a book's publication—is an obvious tipoff that a dust jacket, if not necessarily the book itself, is not of the first state. But apart from memorization, there's no way to know every case.

For instance, here's the jacket flap of the first edition of Gabriel García Márquez's 1970 novel *One Hundred Years of Solitude*.

The first printing of the jacket has an exclamation point at the end of the lead paragraph of the front flap rather than the period shown here. What's the difference between the DJ states worth to a collector? Maybe $1,200—quite a lot for an exclamation point!

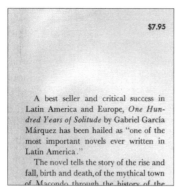
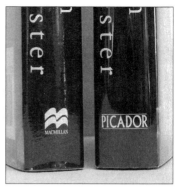

A best seller and critical success in Latin America and Europe, *One Hundred Years of Solitude* by Gabriel García Márquez has been hailed as "one of the most important novels ever written in Latin America."

The novel tells the story of the rise and fall, birth and death, of the mythical town of Macondo through the history of the

$7.95

It's perhaps unnecessary but nevertheless important to note that while this kind of is-there-an-exclamation-point? distinction warrants careful scrutiny when you're considering a $1,000 auction bid on a first edition of *One Hundred Years of Solitude*, if you run across a copy at a yard sale, just hand over the one or two bucks, walk away quickly, and look it over more closely once you're safely at home.

And sometimes the first-printing question comes down to not differences in the text but in the imprint: One publisher's copies will hit bookstore shelves before another's, which matters to some collectors.

Consider John Lanchester's marvelous culinary murder mystery *The Debt to Pleasure*. The 1996 U.S. first is fairly common, but I wanted a British first, since it was printed a year earlier and features a lovely design. But Picador, the U.K. publisher, complicated things: It changed the imprint of about a third of the book's ten thousand first printing from *Picador* to *Macmillan*, designating the Macmillan copies for sale in Australia and New Zealand. It was *those* copies that actually went on sale first, making the Macmillan edition the book's true first—even though, since Lanchester is English, some collectors prefer the U.K. first as a matter of principle.

For a few more examples, check out the "Bibliographic/News Notes" page on the website of Santa Monica, California, bookseller Barry R. Levin. We learn there, for instance, that "the true world first edition" of Stephen King's novel *Dolores Claiborne* was an Australian book-

**What's the Point of "Points"?**
(*above left*) A $1,200 point: If that period were an exclamation point, this 1970 first edition of *One Hundred Years of Solitude* would be worth about $1,500 instead of $300. Too bad.

**What's the Point of "Points"?**
(*above right*) The first-printing mystery: The U.K. and Australian editions of John Lanchester's 1995 novel *The Debt to Pleasure*. Which is the true first?

club copy "issued just one day before the early release of the British trade edition in Australia, nine days before the British 'Special Limited Christmas Edition,' ten days before the [American] Stephen King Bookclub edition, and very clearly before the American trade hardcover edition."

What this means is that if you decide you want the best possible copy of *Dolores Claiborne*, you'll have to track one down from an Australian dealer.

**Beyond Firsts.** From hardcover first edition to pocketbook to movie tie-in.

## Beyond Firsts: From ARCs to BCEs

Collecting doesn't begin and end with first editions. Most books of any significance whatsoever will appear in more than one edition, including some or all of these, in order: galley, advance copy, limited edition, first edition, book-club edition, trade-paperback reprint, and pocketbook reprint—and each of these in different countries.

As long as there's interest in a book, its publisher will do everything it can to prolong its life, through repackaging and republication, working to get it in front of as many potential buyers as possible. For instance, a new film adaptation of a book, whether originally published last year or a century go, will surely inspire a new edition featuring the lead actors on the cover. If the film is a hit, the publisher may bring out all the author's work again in a uniform edition whose design invokes the film.

As a guideline, the further a copy is from the first edition, the less desirable it is as a collectible. As with everything involving books, there are plenty of exceptions, of course: No one knows what will happen years from now—which books, in which editions, will be prized, or common, or rare, or utterly forgotten.

There are always quirks. Allen and Patricia Ahearn note the odd fact that sometimes limited editions are actually easier to find than first editions of the same book, even when many more copies of the latter were published. Why? Because the people who buy and own the limited editions are far more likely to keep and preserve their books. The counterintuitive result is that a signed first from an edition of 10,000 copies may, fifty years later, be scarcer and more valuable than a book from a five-hundred-copy signed edition.

It's this kind of peculiarity, of course, that keeps book collecting interesting.

## Take It to the Limited

In a sense, every first edition is a limited edition, published in a finite number. But what is meant by *limited editions* are those set apart from the regular first, intended to be collectibles from the outset. (Some collectors avoid limited editions altogether, dubbing them "manufactured rarities" or "created collectibles.") Whether they're signed and numbered or plain, in editions of ten or ten thousand, limited editions are special. That doesn't necessarily mean they're rare, or of great lasting value, or even more desirable than regular trade editions, but they're exclusive by virtue of being, well, limited.

The most recognizable and commonly seen limited editions are those published by the Franklin Mint, which focuses on literary titles, some of them signed true first editions. They're not necessarily rare—some titles get relatively large printings—but Franklin copies of important books are always of value. (A few novels that don't catch on, like Louis Auchincloss's 1983 novel *Exit Lady Masham*, John Gregory Dunne's 1994 novel *Playland*, and Muriel Spark's 1984 novel *The Only Problem*, can be had for under $20, but that's unusual.) Often the copyright page will state, "This Limited First Edition has been privately printed, and personally signed by . . . exclusively for the members of The Signed First Edition Society."

Another recognizable series is the books published by the Limited Editions Club. Founded in 1929, the club has produced a wide range of titles, issued in fine bindings and slipcases, with most limited to 1,500 copies of each edition. The club's unsigned books aren't necessarily all that valuable—you can find some in the $10-to-$20 range—and there are even bargains on books signed by the illustrator. Others, though, are quite valuable—and that's not even taking into account the 1935 edition of

*Ulysses* signed and numbered by both James Joyce and Henri Matisse. They're usually reissues of classic titles and therefore not first editions, but they're lovely nevertheless. Similarly, the Easton Press focuses on "the world's greatest books"—lovely leatherbound, gilt-edged volumes intended to last a lifetime or more.

Franklin, Limited Editions Club, and Easton books are expensive to buy new, and they look and feel expensive—not to mention distinctive. All of which means that you're unlikely to find them at yard sales for 50 cents each. Indeed, that's true of limited editions in general—they look different and, more important, are initially distributed to people who either keep them (friends of the author, galleries, etc.) or who sell high-level books professionally. If you want them, fine, but you're unlikely to get a bargain. There's no ignorance gap when you buy from a dealer—you can't assume that you know more than he does.

The Heritage Press, an offshoot of the Limited Editions Club, publishes books that look as though they're limited but aren't, and they're correspondingly more common and less valuable, though still quite attractive. Heritage books are like issues of *National Geographic* in that subscribers end up with a ton of them and the books often have little resale value—even though they *feel* like things that should be treasured. The result is bookstore rows of low-priced, slipcased copies of titles like Herman Melville's *Omoo* and William Thackeray's *The Newcomes*—that is, books that hardly anyone reads anymore. If you're genuinely interested, go for it, but don't buy just because they look like bargains.

Regular trade publishers occasionally bring out limited editions of books by popular authors, to offer something special to fans who would otherwise be able to buy only the same book as 499,999-odd other readers. The editions usually have different bindings and/or slipcases, have higher cover prices than the regular firsts, and are far harder to get—indeed, you often have to order them through new bookstores, and that's after you even find out they're scheduled for publication.

Some trade-publisher limited editions have stair-step levels: for instance, twenty-six lettered copies, one hundred signed and numbered copies, and five hundred unnumbered copies. Obviously, in this case, the signed and numbered copies are worth more than the plain ones, and the lettered copies are worth still more. It shouldn't make a difference, but collectors prefer lower numbers (and letters) to higher ones.

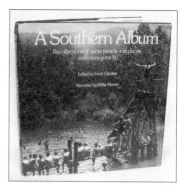

Not all limited trade editions are signed, and not all are as limited as in this example. To accompany its 6.8 million first editions of *Harry Potter and the Order of the Phoenix*, Scholastic published 350,000 copies of a slipcased, $60 "Deluxe Edition." That's far more, of course, than all but a relative handful of *regular* editions, meaning that you can't count on even the limited-edition copies retaining their value.

**Take it to the Limited.** Not so limited: One of 50,000—count 'em, 50,000—signed and numbered copies of this 1975 book.

Even signed and numbered copies aren't necessarily rare, and they're certainly not always valuable. Here's one you may run across, an attractive, oversize volume of prose and photographs from 1975. But look more closely at the autographed bookplate inside, and you learn that this is one of *fifty thousand* signed copies! Not surprisingly, it's not worth much—about half, in fact, of what it sold for new almost three decades ago.

## Looking Fine

The *really* unusual limited editions you'll occasionally see are published by small presses and "fine" presses. These are the ones that'll bring out an edition of ten copies, or fifty, and that's it. They may be on handmade paper, or in an odd size, or even in an unusual shape.

In the 1920s, with the economy booming, the book-buying public showed interest in limited editions, and publishers obliged, producing an unusual number of slipcased and finely bound mail-order books in series of 500 to 1,500 copies each, largely of what twenties publisher Donald Friede dubbed "polite erotica."

(Most of these titles, I should interject, have little merit in a strictly literary sense, confirming the persuasive argu-

**Looking Fine.**
Signed limited editions of 250 (John L'Heureux) and 225 copies (Christopher Buckley) each.

ment that author J. Herbert Slater offered in 1905: "Books extensively advertised as being issued in limited editions should be avoided, for no publisher would appeal to a small audience if he were sure of a large one.")

Since then, poetry collections have been perhaps the most common titles to appear in fine-press editions, for two reasons: There's rarely a demand for tens of thousands of copies of any particular book of poetry, and collections usually have comparatively few pages and sparse text, making them more amenable to unusual formatting and materials. But you can find other genres: short stories, essays, novel fragments, even full-length novels.

Indeed, perhaps the best-known limited editions are those written by the prolific novelists John Updike and Stephen King, each of whom have generated a wide variety of hard-to-find books for small publishers in addition to their prodigious trade-edition output. Updike has been bringing out curious volumes since the 1960s; King has offered special editions of his novels since becoming a best-seller machine in 1980.

In March 2003, an eBay seller offered the "holy grail of Stephen King collectibles": one of twenty-six lettered copies of an aluminum-covered-asbestos edition of his novel *Firestarter*. The opening bid was $6,000, and the bidding topped out at $12,651.

Think about it: $12,651, for a book—a pretty darn cool book, but a book not even twenty-five years old. A book by *Stephen King*, who even fans acknowledge isn't exactly Flaubert. For about the same amount, you could buy a first American edition of Charles Darwin's *On the Origin of Species*, or a first of Harriet Beecher Stowe's *Uncle Tom's Cabin*, or a first of Dashiell Hammett's *The Maltese Falcon*. Or, come to think of it, a late-model-year Honda Civic.

However rare, is this book really worth $12,651? I asked the buyer, a British business owner named Jason Canny, who didn't find the question particularly difficult: "The reason I paid such a high price for this edition of *Firestarter*??? Simply, I am a King completist, and this edition was the final 'piece in the jigsaw'—I now own every U.S. and U.K. first edition and all the limited editions."

It's hard to argue with a completist, particularly one so devoted and monomaniacal as to take on the voluminous works of Stephen King. Congratulations to Jason are in order!

Under limited editions, I should also mention *broadsides*, which are single-sided sheets, typically of a poem or very short story and usually printed attractively on heavy stock. Some well-known writers (including Richard Brautigan and Charles Bukowski) printed broadsides early in their careers; those can be quite valuable, since few have survived. What you're more likely to run across are items by established writers that are printed to commemorate occasions or simply as desirable limited items.

**Looking Fine—Broadsides.** A poem and short story printed on single sheets, in broadside format.

## Where Do Advance Copies Come From?

You're not supposed to be able to buy pre-publication copies of books. No one is—that's why publishers put "Not for Sale" and "For Promotional Purposes Only" on the back. You'll never see one at a Borders.

So how do advance copies get out in the world? And what are they, anyway?

Publishers print them for, well, promotional purposes. They're mailed to bookstore owners, chain-store buyers, and book reviewers at newspapers, magazines, and, increasingly, websites; they're handed out at conventions like the giant BookExpo America and regional conferences and fairs; they're sent to prominent friends of the author in hopes of procuring a blurb to put on the finished book's dust jacket. The idea is to create buzz, to get a book into the hands of people who will tell poten-

**Where do Advance Copies Come From?** Galleys, proofs, and ARCs.

tial buyers about it. But once the tastemakers have taken a look, they don't need their advance copies anymore—unless they're collectors, of which there are comparatively few in the publishing industry. Those extra copies end up donated, at local stores (most notably at New York's legendary Strand), sold online, or thrown in the trash.

People use the terms *galleys, proofs,* and *advance copies* interchangeably, but they refer to different things: *Bound galleys* are plain copies of books printed early in the editing process, before the author has made revisions. *Uncorrected proofs* are typically printed after author revisions but before final formatting. *Advance reading copies* (ARCs for short) are very similar to the book that will eventually hit store shelves, usually with illustrated covers that may or may not resemble the finished cover design. All these states are generally softcovers, sent out months before the on-sale date.

The earliest copies get sent to the most important reviewers, at publications like *The New York Times,* and to the top store buyers; ARCs go to anyone in the industry who might read the book and talk about it. Not all books get advance copies in the first place—review copies are just regular first editions, packaged with a press release or two—and only a few go through the galley, proof, *and* ARC stages.

The first ARCs appeared in the 1930s; by the 1950s, publishers had fully embraced the idea; by the early 1980s, collectors had begun to recognize their potential value. Indeed, advance copies of significant books can be desirable collectibles: They're not widely available, they appear *before* the true first, and there usually are far fewer of them than the trade edition. Most plain galleys you'll see, from major publishers, get print runs of 100 to 200 copies. Small publishers may produce as few as a dozen copies—or none at all.

ARCs, with close-to-final text and attractively designed covers, are much more common: Publishers may print as many as 5,000 and send them to each Barnes & Noble, Borders, independent bookstore . . . you can see how the numbers add up. This also explains why a debut novel that fails to catch on may turn up more often in ARC form than in first edition: After the unsold hardcovers are remaindered or pulped, there may actually be more copies of the ARC in circulation.

In spring 2003, Doubleday gambled by printing some ten thousand glossy ARCs of Dan Brown's novel *The Da Vinci Code*—an expensive proposition, considering that none of those copies would put any money in the publisher's pocket. (It paid off: Booksellers loved the novel and helped make it a surprise best-seller.)

You'll run across advance copies at bookstores and sales, more often if you're in a big city and *much* more often if you're in New York, the center of the publishing world. Since at certain stores you can find a pretty much unlimited number of ARCs at a very low price, it's tempting to sweep up all you can, at least of first novels. (For whatever reason, advance copies of nonfiction books—even of titles that go on to be best-sellers and win prizes—are rarely worth anything at all.) But advance copies have no inherent value; unless the author turns out to be significant, you may end up with moldering boxes of anonymous softcovers, worth nothing to anyone save the author and his parents. On the other hand, it's likely that a few of the books *will* be significant, in which case your investment—literary or economic—may pay off in the long run.

It's worth noting that many collectors shun advance copies altogether, and that there's no rule at all about whether an ARC is worth more or less than the same book's first edition. Some are; some aren't.

Now, the question implied at the beginning of this section: Is it unethical to buy and sell advance copies? After all, neither the publisher nor the author makes a dime when an ARC is sold.

The issue predates ARCs altogether. Around the time of the Civil War, according to publishing historian John Tebbel, publishers sent out a tremendous number of review copies—"a considerable part of the entire first edition"—in hopes of eliciting writeups in newspapers and magazines, which devoted far more space to book reviews than they do today. The editors receiving the books, predictably, saw them as "a rather profitable source of revenue" and resold their extras, confusing the market and annoying booksellers. The introduction of ARCs helped solve that problem, since the softcovers couldn't be resold as regular first editions.

How do the authors feel about ARCs being collectibles? I've found most, when presented with them at a signing, to be either enthusiastic (Jim Lehrer: "Wow—I've never even *seen* these before!") or at worst blasé ("You got this at the Strand, didn't you?"). A few have taken a public stand against their sale; novelist T.C. Boyle, for instance, explains on his website why he refuses to autograph them: "I'll sign all commercial editions, but decline only to sign advance readers' copies because those are given away free and then become objects of greed for certain sellers and collectors." Publicists, quite naturally, frown on the resale of their promotional tools.

In *Selling Used Books Online*, Stephen Windwalker notes that Amazon.com sternly forbids its sellers from offering ARCs—but that "thousands" are offered regardless. Publishers' efforts to control their distribution, he writes, "have been utterly futile."

Technology may soon make the whole issue moot: In 2002, publishers began experimenting with electronic editions of advance copies, which solves the problem of getting the copies in front of the right people's eyes and saves money—after all, ARCs cost the publisher perhaps $10 each to produce. But it'll be a while yet: Few readers so far have shown themselves willing to swap actual books for onscreen text, no matter how convenient. Reviewers and publishing-industry people are no exception.

## Don't Join the Club: Watching Out for BCEs

It's the single most common mistake that novice book-buyers and -sellers make: thinking that a book-club edition is the real thing. Often the mistake is an easy one to make—the books can look just like firsts, with only tiny clues to distinguish them. Other times, it's obvious.

Either way, BCEs are the bane of collectors. They're almost universally shunned, and their very existence can be frustrating: You may frequently run across nice copies of early novels by the likes of Toni Morrison and Anne Tyler, whose first editions are often quite valuable, and discover that all of them are BCEs. Indeed, many '60s and '70s hardcovers are far more common in BCE than in trade editions; among the notable ones you may encounter more often than you'd like: Heinrich Böll's *Group Portrait With Lady*, Annie Dillard's *Pilgrim at Tinker Creek*, William Gaddis' *J R*, John Irving's *The World According to Garp*, John Nichols' *The Sterile Cuckoo*, and Jacqueline Susann's *Valley of the Dolls*. You might open up fifty hardcover copies of Jack Finney's novel *Time and Again* before finding one first edition.

It's worth asking: Why are BCEs to be avoided, particularly since some resemble first editions in almost every way?

Some critics point to the noticeably inferior materials and production of most BCEs. Still, considering that many Book-of-the-Month Club editions are nearly identical to the true firsts, materials can't explain all the difference. So perhaps the primary reason is that while trade editions have finite printings—meaning that they can become scarce—BCEs can be reprinted in unlimited quantities, for years after the book's original publication. No mismatch between supply and demand = no collectibility.

Determining whether a book is a BCE is often easy, and it gets easier with practice. Sometimes you can tell just by the shininess of the dust jacket; with a few titles, you'll have to open to see whether there's a price printed on

the flap. (Since the books aren't sold in stores, they don't have printed prices.)

With books published in the last forty years, you'll most commonly run across two BCE types: Literary Guild and Book-of-the-Month Club. The companies were founded in the 1920s, when the publishing industry included many book clubs, and continue to thrive.

**Watching Out for BCEs.** No jacket-flap price? Probably a book-club edition.

The easy ones to tell are those published by the Literary Guild after World War II: They're smaller in format, thinner, printed on cheap paper, with easily rubbed and torn covers. Open one, and the jacket flap has no price and—I told you this was easy—"Book Club Edition" printed at the bottom. With a little practice, you'll be able to run your fingers over a row of Literary Guild BCEs and tell without even pulling any of them out. "[A] book club book simply feels wrong," writes *Book Finds* author Ian C. Ellis.

When Literary Guild books are missing DJs, it's a little harder to tell, but you'll soon have those down pretty well too: The BCEs skimp on design and production—one-color boards instead of two-tone, blind-stamped author's initials rather than gilt. In addition, copyright pages lack the telltale first-edition points. (Not only that—you shouldn't be looking to buy books without DJs in the first place!)

Book-of-the-Month Club (BOMC) selections are far more difficult to spot. Most of the time, they're the same size; the boards and paper are the same material; and even the copyright pages can be identical. And there's no helpful "Book Club Edition" note.

The two primary tipoffs: There's no price on the jacket flap, and there's a *blind stamp* on the back board. Most of the time—though certainly not all—the copyright page indicates that a BCE is a generic later printing, not a first. (Some recent copies add a BOMC promotional statement to the bottom of the copyright page.)

The blind stamp is something that non-collectors rarely know about. It's a small impression on the back of the book itself, under the dust jacket. Usually the stamp is in the shape of a square, though in past years BOMC has used a circle or even, in the forties and fifties, a white dot or pinprick hole.

As with everything else in book collecting, exceptions abound. In the mid-1970s, a few publishers seemingly set out to confuse collectors: Their BCEs began stating on the copyright page that they were first editions. One reason why it's so frustrating to find so many BCEs of *Pilgrim at Tinker Creek* and *J R* and Martin Amis's *The Rachel Papers* is that their copyright pages *say* they're firsts even when they're not.

**Watching Out for BCEs— Size Matters.** Trade and book-club editions of Pat Conroy's 1986 novel *The Prince of Tides*.

It often happens, then, that an amateur online bookseller (not to mention some unscrupulous pros) will list a 1970s first edition that is in actuality a BCE. It doesn't hurt to double-check by asking questions before an auction closes or a purchase is finalized. Likewise, in a bookstore or at a sale, it takes only a few seconds to peek under the DJ to see if there's a blind stamp.

Are no BCEs worth anything at all? Well, some are worth *something*. Postwar Literary Guild copies are pretty much always worthless, but pre-1960 BOMC copies that match trade editions carry some value, when the original book is comparatively valuable and/or scarce.

The BCEs that really *should* have some value but don't are those for which the edition was the only hardcover published. You'll run across these most often when perusing theatrical plays and science-fiction novels. Apart from theater-club hardcovers and the occasional trade paperback, plays usually appear only in thin, paper-

covered actor's editions. (A relative handful, by major playwrights, get regular hardcover printings.) Sci-fi novels of the 1960s and 1970s frequently entered the world as pocketbook originals, and BCEs were the sole hardcover printings.

I wouldn't count on these books *ever* becoming valuable in collectors' eyes, so don't accumulate them with investment in mind. But those collecting them are certainly appreciative of the low prices!

**Watching Out for BCEs—The Blind Stamp.** The hidden indentation on the back of a BOMC edition.

## The Second Time Around

Remember these names: Triangle. Sun Dial. A.L. Burt. Tower. Blue Ribbon. Blakiston. Grosset & Dunlap. They're reprint publishers—companies that published inexpensive editions of best-sellers—and if you're looking for books published in the first half of the twentieth century, you'll run across those names constantly. (There's more about book clubs and reprint publishers in Chapter Three.)

Though they were often distributed through mail-order book clubs, reprint copies aren't the same as BCEs: They bear their own publisher imprints, while BCEs retain the marks of the original publishers. But they have no price on the jacket flap, and they're often published on cheaper, thinner paper, with less sturdy binding.

Only infrequently do the books have much value to serious collectors, which opens up a real opportunity for the person interested in finding multiple editions of favorite authors and books. The exceptions are with trade books that are truly hard to find—their reprint copies may carry some value—and with reprints that have dazzling dust jackets promoting a film adaptation.

By and large, unless you find the books already bearing nice DJs, and unless you're collecting different copies of particular books and authors, you should avoid reprint editions. With popular authors, you can often find the true first editions for the same price, and there's no rea-

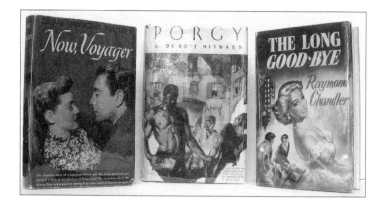

son to settle for a second-best copy. Plus, you'd be surprised how little most reprint copies—even with nice jackets—are worth on the open market.

**The Second Time Around.** Some reprint editions have lovely dust jackets.

How do you tell a reprint copy? As with all book IDs, it's not as easy as you might hope. Those names I mentioned are a giveaway, though there are always exceptions. For instance, Grosset & Dunlap, which sold books mostly through drugstores, wasn't *strictly* a reprint publisher—the company published some original novels by the likes of Zane Grey.

It's important to note that almost all of the reprint publishers (Tower and World are notable exceptions) use misleading copyright pages—there's often no more information than the original trade edition, implying that the reprint is a first or, at the least, a recent later printing. In fact, a Grosset & Dunlap book may have been published years later; the only way to tell when is by checking the list of also-by titles—obviously, a copy that lists later books in a series postdates the original publication of those books.

As an example, let's say you're looking for a nice copy of Eleanor H. Porter's classic children's novel *Pollyanna*. In February 1913, the book appeared under the imprint of L.C. Page & Co. But two other publishers—G&D and A.L. Burt—soon got into the act. Their editions of *Pollyanna* bear no other dates than 1913, and their dust jackets carry different designs altogether. If you run across one of these reprint copies, there's almost nothing to indicate that it's less collectible than the Page edition.

Hence the reason to familiarize yourself with the publishers—and if you're collecting, in this case, early-twentieth-century children's books, with the different editions you may encounter.

The heyday of reprint publishers ended in the 1940s, but some still produce work. Greenwood and Praeger, for instance, keep in print old African-American and academic books that otherwise would be virtually unavailable. Even if the copies aren't exactly collectible, they're of great value to readers.

Incidentally, those hardcover *Reader's Digest* editions that compile several novels in a single volume are *never* worth anything (with the exception of the very first volume, from 1941). If you end up with any—unavoidably, I hope—just donate 'em.

### Following the Flag: Books of the World

Most collectors prefer firsts published in the author's home country, a pattern that collectors dub "following the flag" (though it's unclear if that phrase has ever appeared anywhere but in books about book collecting). What this means is that there's a real opportunity to snatch up interesting and unusual copies of favorite titles at low prices by *not* following the flag.

Considering their relative scarcity, many foreign editions seem downright bargains. Look at Barbara Kingsolver's 1988 debut, *The Bean Trees*. In England, Virago published just 1,250 copies of the book, a lovely little hardcover featuring completely different artwork and design than the U.S. version. It's much scarcer and—here's the key—perhaps a sixth of the price. If you're a Kingsolver fan and aren't quite willing to drop $250 on the true first of *The Bean Trees*, the Virago edition is a terrific substitute. If you're fortunate enough to already own the U.S. edition, the U.K. edition would make a great shelf companion.

Likewise, Cormac McCarthy's 1992 novel *All the Pretty Horses*, whose U.K. first printing was 4,000 copies, one-fifteenth as many as published here, but is still much cheaper. There are any number of examples. U.S. publishers print many more copies of particular titles than those in smaller countries, so the books are de facto scarcer.

They also frequently look quite different: When a book's rights in the United States and England belong to different publishers, the two editions' size and cover design may bear no resemblance. A hardcover on these shores may appear as a softcover there. Even the title may change—abbreviated, tweaked, or replaced altogether.

Even Canadian editions sometimes carry different dust-jacket designs, and with Canadian authors (e.g., Margaret Atwood, Robertson Davies, or Rohinton Mistry) that one is the more desirable copy.

And you needn't stop with the countries of the English-speaking world. There's a whole world of books out there—literally—and it's worth exploring. With the Internet, international book shopping doesn't even require plane fare to Spain or Australia. Tracking down and ordering favorite books online from faraway booksellers can be exciting, from trying to translate descriptions of Italian or German editions to seeing what the books actually look like when they arrive. (In America, of course, most of us know only English and aren't particularly tolerant of others' reluctance to speak it. Think twice before you start sending impatient e-mails asking some French bookseller to clarify whether Tom Wolfe's *Le bûcher des vanités* is a first edition and whether the corners show any shelfwear.)

Be prepared for extra charges—at the end of the process of ordering, say, Swedish books, you may be asked to pay what seem like extraordinarily high tariffs. Is it worth it? You'll have to decide for yourself, book by book.

Besides the uncertainty, the only problem with buying foreign books is that, more than likely, you can't read

**Following the Flag.** Foreign publishers offer unusual editions of familiar books.

**Following the Flag—For Completists Only.** German, U.S., and British first editions of Mark Helprin's 1977 novel *Refiner's Fire*.

them. (My wife was less than pleased when my first purchase in German arrived in the mail.) But there's a good argument to be made (at least I thought so) that even if the collectible book were in English it would be staying on the shelf anyway—you weren't going to be leafing through it on the subway or at the beach.

If you can track down different editions of favorite books, you may find yourself with a marvelous—and almost completely unique—set of volumes. "People do like non-U.S. editions of favorite books, but not as many people are completists as there used to be," says Ken Gloss of Brattle Book Shop. "People are more interested in high spots"—that is, in a book's true first edition, regardless of nationality, and that's it.

## Who'd Pay Money for *This*?: Supply and Demand

It's not enough that a book is old.

Or that it's a first edition.

Or that has a cool cover.

Or that it sold a ton of copies.

Or that it won a big literary prize.

First principle: For a book to have any value at all, new or used, there must be a market for it. That is, someone has to want to buy it.

As with the price of most things in this world, the value of a book is founded on supply and demand. That means that for a book to be considered collectible, more people must want copies than there *are* copies. Their level of desire for copies (demand) meets the supply (the number of available copies), and the value stabilizes. If a cheaper copy appears on the markets, falling below a potential buyer's personal price point, he'll snap it up. If a more expensive one appears, he won't.

That personal price point—multiplied by the number of people looking for the book, forming a consensus—represents the book's true value.

Now, since there are so many variables involved in any given book—condition, edition, etc.—and with that author and title compared to the millions of others, the value isn't fixed. *Not at all.* Sure, with a handful of "high points" collectibles—Poe, Shakespeare, etc.—serious collectors are generally aware of most of the copies in existence, how much someone paid for them last time they came up at auction, and how much they might go for *next* time they're available. But with everything else, the market is completely fluid. The well-received publication of a new biography of an author may suddenly raise the value of her books; an author's disastrous second novel may deflate enthusiasm for his debut; several collectors' decision to sell their prizes may throw the market into temporary chaos.

All the fluctuation helps keep the hobby fun: A book you pay $20 for may be worth $100 next year . . . or $5. You may be able to sell another book for more than you thought it was worth. There's the inevitable disappointment of firing up the computer and learning that the promising-looking first edition of Camus' *Resistance, Rebellion, and Death* you uncovered at the bookstore is worth no more than the $10 you paid. But then there's the elation of discovering that the copy of *Valley of the Dolls* that you picked up as a joke is a $100 book.

### "Are My Old Books Worth Anything?"
I dread getting this question, since the answer almost never makes anyone happy. Old books turn up all the time—in attics, buried on shelves, in parents' basements—and they look as though they *must* be worth something to someone.

They bear famous names—George Eliot, Edgar Allan Poe, Lord Byron, Charles Dickens, Guy de Maupassant, O. Henry, H.G. Wells—and even well-known titles. These are novels and stories that are still read today, from *Anna Karenina* to *Frankenstein* to *Sense and Sensibility*. They're a century or so old, with attractive covers, in decent shape, without even a musty odor—why *wouldn't* they be worth something?

Well, first of all, they're almost certainly not first editions.

**Are My Old Books Worth Anything?** Umm … probably not. Sorry.

They're likely not even *early* editions. These classic titles were published in dozens of different forms by a variety of publishers—and they're *still* being published today. Any serious collector looking for high-grade copies of Hardy or Thackeray or Tolstoy isn't all that interested in reprints, unless they're special illustrated or signed and limited editions. So if you're hoping to fatten your toddler's college fund by selling those pretty John Galsworthy volumes, you're likely to be disappointed.

But if you're looking to *buy* nice old books, it's a different story.

The silver lining is, once again, opportunity. If you're a fan of Dickens or Dumas and can't afford to spend thousands at auctions on early English copies of *The Pickwick Papers* or *The Count of Monte Cristo*, you can fairly easily and inexpensively begin compiling a collection of lovely old editions.

Indeed, the books you can get cheap usually have covers far more ornate and attractive than the original publications, most of which are dull and small-format. As John Carter notes in *Taste & Technique in Book Collecting*, many first editions—he cites as examples some seventeenth- and eighteenth-century classics—are "conspicuously lacking in physical appeal to the uninitiated eye." Many early novels were first published in small formats and multiple volumes, without attractive cover designs or materials.

And not to dampen your enthusiasm, but truly valuable firsts of antiquarian classics are just plain unlikely to turn up in an attic. That's not to say it's impossible—in 1925, an elderly widow discovered a copy of Edgar Allan Poe's impossibly rare *Tamerlane and Other Poems* in her house, and in the late 1980s a fisherman found a copy of the same book in a New Hampshire antiques shop. But don't get your hopes up too high.

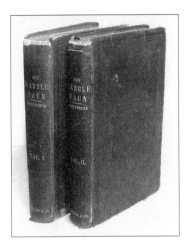

This admonishment, incidentally, is aimed directly at novice eBay sellers who write wide-eyed descriptions of "first editions" of the likes of Victor Hugo or Washington Irving, with item photographs depicting 1930s reprints. Sometimes the books are listed as "signed" as well, based on the facsimile scrawl under the author photo— though a quick Google search turns up the unfortunate fact of the author's death in, say, 1824.

In any case, there's nothing wrong with devoting a shelf—a short one, ideally—to your grandmother's favorite old books, regardless of whether you could get anything for them on eBay. That's why the term *sentimental value* was coined.

**Are My Old Books Worth Anything?**—"Lacking in Physical Appeal." An 1860 first edition of Nathaniel Hawthorne's *The Marble Faun*—not exactly a feast for the senses.

## What Does *Rare* Mean?

On eBay, *rare* refers to anything that's neither brand-new nor flea-market common. On the Universal Rarity Scale—developed by twenty-one experts in 1998 to define rarity in any field—an item is truly rare if only a handful are known to exist. For book-collecting purposes, the real definition is somewhere in between: a book that you're unlikely to run across without looking hard—and that is genuinely collectible.

Just as it's not enough for a book to be old, it's not enough for it to be uncommon. No matter how few copies of a book were printed, it's of no value unless someone wants it. In fact, some won't even use the word *rare* to characterize used books that have no demand—they substitute the word *secondhand*. (Author and bookseller Stephen Windwalker proposes a fresh set of categories for used books: hyper-common, outdated, common, uncommon, scarce, and rare.)

Of course, whether you consider a book uncommon is somewhat subjective: In his 1904 *The Book-Collector*, W. Carew Hazlitt insisted that collectors of the day were overvaluing certain desirable volumes: "There are rare books which, paradoxical as it may seem, are not rare," he writes. Among the seventeenth-century books he lists are the Shakespeare First Folio and the first editions of John Milton's *Paradise Lost* and John Bunyan's *Pilgrim's Progress*. Even the Gutenberg Bible, he suggests, is not actually rare: "at least forty must exist . . . throughout the world." Somewhat surprisingly, Nicholas Basbanes, in *Among the Gently Mad*, agrees: "[I]s this a rare book? Relatively speaking, no."

But surely this is a standard of rarity that few today can afford to adhere to, considering that a copy of the Gutenberg Bible is worth around $20 million and that forty copies (Basbanes lists forty-seven) doesn't sound like a whole lot. At the least, it puts in perspective those collectors who fill shelves with glossy first editions of 500,000-first-printing novels.

With regard to value, the supply-and-demand issue is most obvious when looking at recent blockbusters. Take Robert James Waller's 1992 blockbuster *The Bridges of Madison County*. Warner Books' first printing was 35,000, comparatively large for a debut novelist, but even so, you could flip open every copy you run across at yard sales and never find one—after all, 35,000 is a small fraction of the book's 12 million hardcover sales.

And yet, think about it: 35,000 copies of the first printing are out there—and there just aren't *that* many people who desire it enough to pay a premium. It's safe to say that most of Waller's millions of readers don't particularly care whether their copy is collectible—particularly now that many of those millions are (justifiably) embarrassed by their initial enthusiasm.

The result is an enormous supply—last time I checked an online listing, booksellers had more than 200 copies of the first printing available—and not all that much demand. While prices range up to $400, you can now score a first for as little as $25—and there's no reason to think that the price won't continue to sink. (Signed copies of Waller's hard-to-find 1988 first book, *Just Beyond the Firelight*, can now be had for well under $100.)

**Book Values 101**

The Internet has allowed a free and transparent market to flourish. With sellers and buyers able to find each other more easily, and with information more widely available than ever before, supply can meet demand, resulting in equilibrium. Right?

Sort of. The problem is that there are in many cases too few examples to allow free-market principles to work, way too many variables (condition, edition, etc.), and no authoritative guide to simply *state* what a book is worth.

Allen and Patricia Ahearn's *Collected Books* lists values, as do several other guides. But prices can change so quickly that you can't take the values—however definitive they appear in the pages of a hardcover book—as more than just guidelines. There's no equivalent of *Beckett Baseball Card Monthly*.

Decades ago, book price guides based their listings on store surveys of how much items had actually been selling for—and that's still the way it's done. But over the course of a year, there just aren't that many individual titles sold, compared to what's out there. *Collected Books* covers more than 20,000 titles—a lot by anyone's standards—and yet that's just the tip of the iceberg. The Library of Congress holds some six million English-language books—and that doesn't include nearly everything ever published in this country. No magazine or reference book could cover more than a tiny fraction of these, not to mention accounting for variations and different editions.

Even the free-market Internet is hardly foolproof when it comes to pricing books. For instance, an online search for an unsigned first edition of Oscar Hijuelos's 1989 Pulitzer-winning novel *The Mambo Kings Play Songs of*

*Love* turns up fine copies for as little as $10 and as much as $100. What's it worth? If you run across a copy for $8 in a bookstore, is it a bargain or not?

The simple answer is that it's "worth" the amount that a price-conscious buyer is willing to pay for it—meaning that it's really a $10 book, not a $100 book.

In the case of the Hijuelos book (a magnificent novel that seems undervalued even considering the book's 40,000-copy first printing), so many people are selling copies that the market has worked—buyers and sellers understand each other. But for less common titles, the Internet can accelerate and even create the overvaluing of a particular book. In *Book Collecting for Fun & Profit*, Bill McBride offers an example of how it happens; I'll paraphrase:

A collector decides to sell a book on Alibris and discovers he's the first to post a copy. Where should he price it? It feels to him like a $25 book—but who's to say it's not worth more? So he lists it at $300, just to see if anyone bites. (Why not?) No one immediately does, but two other sellers appear, drawn by the new listing and the prospect of making a quick bundle; they'd rather pocket $200 or so than hold on to their copies of the book. To make their copies seem more appealing, they undercut the original seller: Theirs go online at $225 and $250.

Now comes the tricky part for you, the buyer. A fourth copy shows up on eBay, with a $25 minimum bid, and you look up the book on ABE to see if it's a deal. Sure looks like it! In fact, you'll go all the way to $50, and be happy to pay it, since that's still less than a quarter of what it's worth. Right?

Keeping the example in mind, answer the question: How much *is* the book worth?

The easy answer, again, is that it's worth what people pay for it. But in this case, potential buyers are working off skewed information—not false, exactly, but hardly grounded in common sense. It'll take time, and more copies entering the market, for the price to settle at a realistic level; until that happens, buyers will surely overpay for the book. "Some boring books can be priced really high," says Eugene Okamoto of Philadelphia-area

Harvest Book Co., "if there's just one copy available online. If another one shows up, the price drops in half. It's pure supply-and-demand."

## What Price This Book?

Here's a tale—a cautionary one—of how this works in the real world:

Browsing eBay in late 1998, I was intrigued by a subject line: "What Price Marriage? 1927-Unusual & Beautiful." The photos showed a small, attractive volume, and the auction started at just a few dollars, so I looked up the book and was startled to discover that *What Price Marriage?* was in fact extremely collectible. It was edited—anonymously—by novelist Katherine Anne Porter, who went on to write several famous books and win the Pulitzer Prize in 1966. Three copies were available online; the cheapest was $450, the most expensive $600.

The eBay seller clearly was unaware of the book's true value, and I hoped that no one else would stumble across the listing and run the same search that I had. As the auction neared an end, another serious bidder showed up, but I still ended up spending less than I was prepared to. The final price: $58.55.

*What Price Marriage?* arrived safely in the mail, as pretty and demure as its photos had promised, and I planned for the day when I would sell it—for $300? $350? $400? A big profit no matter what.

Last year I looked up the book again on ABE and found that the playing field had shifted. One seller had cranked it all the way up to $790—wow!—and noted that the book was "Very Hard to find." But clearly that was no longer quite the case: Six others were offering copies. I could now buy a decent copy—from a legitimate dealer rather than some anonymous eBayer in Illinois—for just $65.

What had changed since 1998? Simply, the supply increased—four more dealers had made their stocks available online—and there was no new demand. Nothing had happened since 1998 to spike fresh interest in Katherine Anne Porter, or in her books, or in 1920s anthologies about marriage. So the value dropped with each new seller until—well, until *What Price Marriage?*

was transformed from a $450 book into a $65 book. (Awfully reminiscent of the stock market, huh?)

And surely that lower price tag more accurately reflects the book's true value; if I had tried selling my copy then for $400 or $350 or even the seeming bargain price of $200, it's unlikely that an eager buyer would have appeared to snap it up. There was no window of opportunity that has since shut, since the entire market for the book appears to have been . . . me.

If I had found the book in a dollar box at a yard sale, I would have been thrilled to learn it was worth $65. Was it worth spending $58.55? I'm less certain. In the end, it's just a pretty little book.

## Going Once, Going Twice

Occasionally you'll see an eBay item description explaining a low minimum-bid amount with the sentence, "I thought I'd let the market decide." It's a great thought. Too bad the market is so erratic about making up its mind. You should *never* rely strictly on online auctions to tell you definitively what a book is worth.

As a gauge of a book's collectibility, eBay is a valuable but deeply flawed tool. How much an item sells for—indeed, whether it sells at all—depends on a host of variables, including who happens to be searching that week, where on the site they're searching, and exactly what they're searching for. Also: the subject line, the way the description is written, the quality of the photo, the apparent credibility of the seller, and most important, chance.

Evidence of this is apparent every day on eBay. You can watch identical copies of a particular book (say, a signed first edition of actress Anne Heche's memoir *Call Me Crazy*) go for $10 one week, $50 the next, and back to $10. Sometimes you can tell why by looking at the item descriptions; other times it makes no sense. Maybe there are two people (on opposite coasts, perhaps) willing to pay any amount for the book—but they're both on vacation this week and nowhere near their computers. Maybe a price-is-no-object buyer wants it for a birthday gift *right now*, driving up the bid price of just one copy.

One week in 1999, while selling the occasional extra book on eBay, I was fortunate to find those two people glued to their screens, checkbooks at the ready. I had picked up an autographed Dale Carnegie self-help book in a flea-market box and put it on eBay with a minimum bid of $4. I figured it might go for $10 or so and was startled when the price rose above that—and kept going. By the closing, the two determined bidders had driven the price up over $120.

Over the next few weeks, I noticed other sellers hastily putting up similar copies in hopes of catching the same wave, but alas, they went for, oh, around $10. Does that mean that my copy was "worth" more? Not at all—I was merely the beneficiary of two people happening across a listing and setting their minds to winning the book. (I felt bad that the auction winner overpaid so dramatically . . . but I cashed the check anyway.)

## The Ignorance Gap

Fundamentally, what you're looking for is to land bargains and avoid rip-offs, and there's only one way to do that: You must know more than the seller. You must exploit the *ignorance gap*. "In nature the bird who gets up earliest catches the most worms," British collector Michael Sadleir wrote in 1930, "but in book-collecting the prizes fall to birds who know worms when they see them."

Some seven decades later, the widest gap appears in online auctions—a surprisingly large percentage of sellers fail to do any research at all on what their books are worth, and possibilities abound for curious and persistent bargain-hunters. (Nicholas Basbanes notes that eBay "offers fantastic opportunities to capitalize on the follies of others.") It is, unfortunately, a gap that will certainly narrow as more and more people take advantage of the information that's easily available on the Internet.

One could argue, in fact, that too many people having too much information hurts a hobby—any hobby—for the non-professional collector. If you were collecting baseball cards in the mid-1980s, you'll recall how the fun went out of that hobby due to two factors: oversupply and, more important, the disappearance of the ignorance gap. There were no widely available price guides for sports cards until the late 1970s, and not until 1984 did the first *Beckett Baseball Card Monthly* appear. But suddenly, around 1986, every flea-marketer with a shoe-box of cards had a Beckett guide, and you could no longer hope to browse a card show or garage sale and come away with a pocketful of steals. Worse, general awareness of cards' potential value skyrocketed, meaning that even people without price guides began assuming that their shoebox of common cards were gems.

Today, there is basically no ignorance gap when it comes to baseball cards (not to mention football, basketball, and hockey cards), and the hobby is no longer one for kids—or amateurs. Everyone knows too much.

With instant access to online bookselling sites and information, there's a danger that books could undergo the same process. Already, bookstores no longer offer much opportunity for strict bargain-hunters: It's safe to assume that just about every store manager in America has Internet access. Even if the shop's inventory isn't listed online with Alibris or Advanced Book Exchange, those services' listings directly influence prices. Owners must assume that customers, too, know what a particular book is worth. In a big shop, you'll find fair prices but few steals. "We assume the walk-in customer is a savvy customer," says Ken Eastman of Moe's Books in Berkeley. "We can't be charging things out of line with the real market value."

The gap is shrinking even with regard to online auctions: As eBay sellers—and buyers—grow in skill and numbers, opportunities will certainly shrink. And even places that you'd think immune to the trend are catching on, with a definite negative impact on fun. "Even at church sales now," says New Jersey bookseller Carey G. Spain, "you'll see people selling books for Internet prices."

But there will likely always be an ignorance gap: Books are almost infinitely more complex, varied, and numerous than baseball cards (or stamps, or coins, or nearly anything else), and far fewer people buy books to collect than do to, well, *read*. Be thankful for that! ◨

# 2

# BECOMING
# AN EXPERT

## Collecting Smart: Strategies for Buying

Where you buy is partly determined by *what* you buy. If you're focusing on signed books, you'll have to stick with online sellers and high-tone bookstores; if you're looking for campy old self-help paperbacks, thrift stores are a good bet; if you want advance reading copies, head for the Internet and big used stores in New York or Los Angeles; if you're trying to find nice old copies of classic novels, you may do well at the flea market.

Always remember that the hunt is part of the fun, and make sure not to aim so high that you'll be either permanently disappointed or driven to shop only at the priciest specialist shops.

In old books about collecting, it's almost *required* that the author complain of skyrocketing prices and a dwindling supply of treasures—in short, that newcomers to the hobby are snatching up all the good stuff and leaving only the overpriced and the hopelessly obscure. In *Books and Bookmen*, published in 1886, Andrew Lang sighed that he "does not book-hunt any more," having tired of sifting through piles of mediocrity. The game of book-hunting, he wrote, "has grown too scarce; the preserves are for the rich; the cheap book-stalls hold little but 'The Death of Abel' and 'Sermons' by the Rev. Josiah Gowles, or 'Charles XII.' by M. de Voltaire. I have ceased to hope for better luck; let younger or more sanguine men pursue the fugitive tract and the rare quarto."

Almost a century later, bookseller Robert A. Wilson basically agreed, insisting that any book collector, novice or veteran, must fill his shelves with offerings from dealers: "Long gone—if they ever existed—are the days when a superior collection could be built by haunting thrift shops and general secondhand bookshops."

But this was a pessimistic view in 1886, and it was in 1980, and it is today—and not only because of eBay. You can find *plenty*.

**Bookstores** are where everything begins. Every book lover knows the experience of happening across a shop that she's never seen before, that she didn't even know was in this neighborhood, that she never would have expected to see on this back road. There's no predicting what's inside: a shelf of fabulous finds, a startlingly comprehensive section of your specialty—or, perhaps, nothing of interest anywhere.

Take it in: Is the "Used Books" awning look weather-beaten or freshly painted? What's in the window display? on the sidewalk dollar rack? Is there a prominent "Books Bought" notice?

Once inside, is there a musty odor? Does the guy behind the counter look like the aging-book-junkie owner, or is it some seven-bucks-an-hour high-school kid? Do the books appear to be carefully categorized or gathered into a few loose sections? Are they alphabetized by author? Do hardcovers have glossy dust-jacket protectors? Is there a glass case for antiquarian volumes?

Pull down a few familiar nearby titles and check the prices—high? low? Will you be done with this place in five minutes (*How on earth does this place stay in business?*) or need the rest of the afternoon (*How on earth have I lived without this place?*) to get through everything?

It seems obvious that bookstores—from Borders megastores to dusty neighborhood independents—should be supported and encouraged, that something irreplaceable is lost when a store closes. But it's worth considering *why*. After all, even the most towering Barnes & Noble store doesn't carry much of what's available on www.barnesandnoble.com, and even the most sprawling used bookstores are missing most of what you can find on Bookfinder.

**Strategies for Buying—Bookstores.** Through the door, shelves groaning with rarely seen treasures—or with overpriced paperbacks. Worth checking out?

Actually, there are any number of reasons to support bookstores—and not just morally but with your hard-earned dollars.

Used bookstores still offer an experience that no other forum can duplicate. They're all about surprise (discovering something you didn't know existed), serendipity (happening across something you knew about but had no expectations of finding), and impulse (buying something you had no intention of buying when you entered the store). "A lot of the fun of collecting is the hunt," says Ken Gloss, owner of Brattle Book Shop in Boston. "It's not just going on your computer for three hours and sending a check and hoping the book is what it seems to be."

At good stores, you're sure to encounter items you haven't seen before, that you didn't know existed, in editions with which you're unfamiliar. You'll get ideas about directions to turn in your collecting. You'll see books that you've passed up buying online and realize how much more appealing they may look in your hands. You already know how some books just *feel* right—how the cover design and dust-jacket texture and back-cover copy and first few paragraphs combine to seem irresistible . . . and how some books, even most books, don't.

What does a "good" store look like? Size doesn't matter as much as you might think: Some large stores are crammed with ragged Literary Guild editions and overfamiliar, overpriced remainders; an under-a-stairwell hole-in-the-wall shop could have a variety of unusual finds or have just inherited someone's entire fascinating collection. The stock in used stores may reflect what people from a certain area are reading, or the personal tastes of the owner.

(In *Biblioholism: The Literary Addiction*, Tom Raabe describes the ideal bookstore as one with flawless categorization, space and patience for obscure titles that sell slowly if at all, and no computer books whatsoever. "In fact, the perfect bookstore owner would not even be aware that the computer has been invented," Raabe writes. "Computer types have their own stores. Let them go there.")

Buying is a tougher decision than browsing. In principle, of course you should support a good store—if no one did, it'd disappear—but you're unlikely to find bargains there. Fair prices, sure, but few steals, particularly on real collectibles. With expenses—rent, utilities, staff—that the home eBayer doesn't have, bookstores can't afford to underprice everyone on everything. Even pocketbooks so common that they pile up at library sales at three for a buck will go for $2.50 or more at a bookstore—less, and it's hardly worth the shelf space. (Coupled with the sagging economy, this predicament is what has led to bookstores across the nation closing, and even the survivors losing a significant amount of their walk-in traffic to the Internet.)

Even so, it can make good sense to buy there rather than waiting till you get home and online. For one thing, you pretty much know what you're getting: What the guy behind the counter puts into the bag is what you'll pull out when you get home. If the corners get bumped or DJ torn, it's no one's fault but your own. And you get it *now*: Is your time so valueless that you'd rather return a book to the shelf and go home to spend twenty minutes on the Internet—not to mention waiting a week or more for delivery—to save a few dollars? "With a bookstore," says Seattle store owner Phil Arundel, "there's no shipping, no delays, no disappointments."

Needless to say, the same goes for new bookstores— where you might find, for instance, copies of this book.

**Internet shops** have changed everything about how collectors buy books. With the advent of the Web and sites such as Bibliofind, you could locate copies of items you'd only dreamed about running across; you didn't have to wait for a call from your local paperback exchange for a used copy of the latest best-seller; you didn't have to trek to antiquarian shows to browse high-level collectibles. A whole world of books was only a few mouse clicks away.

It's a reasonable assumption that every single major bookseller in America is now online, with either an individual website or a presence on a site such as Advanced Book Exchange (ABE). That's pretty great in itself—think of how long it'd take to visit each brick-and-mortar store in person—but it's only the beginning of what's available on the Internet for collectors. People finding themselves with a handful, or a hundred, or a thousand books to sell are heading online, meaning that countless books that never otherwise would have been for sale anywhere are now available—to you, and the world.

Where to look? My favorite sites are ABE—I like the interface and find that most online sellers list books on that site—and AddALL, which makes an even broader sweep of books available online. But we're talking about the Internet, so who knows? A week after this book goes to press, both sites could vanish altogether, or a new catch-all site could appear to make all others obsolete. Look around and try different sites; search for the same title on several different sites and see what comes up.

There are two main drawbacks to buying online, one general and one specific:

- Unlike browsing in a bookstore, to find a book on an Internet site you have to know what you're looking for. Perhaps more important, you don't run across items that you're *not* looking for.

- Since in most cases you can't see even pictures of the book before buying, your purchase has two question marks—condition and edition.

I'll talk about condition in more detail later this chapter; for now, know that determining and labeling the shape that a book is in is both subjective and inconsistent. Even pro sellers may not follow accepted guidelines, and amateurs are all over the lot. And then there's shipping. Some sellers toss a book in an unpadded manila envelope, no matter the value; others will lavish extraordinary care on a $1 book, with foam peanuts and layers of bubble wrap. A book may arrive at your door with bumped corners or a crumpled jacket flap, knocking down its condition from fine to very good and its value by half. This is particularly true when it comes to books that the seller doesn't know are collectible—that is, the level of collectible books we're primarily looking at. Your expectations should be higher for more valuable items—after all, when you spend $200 on a book from a capital-B Bookstore, it had *better* show up in the same condition as it left.

In terms of edition—specifically, calling a book a first edition—neither amateurs nor pros are particularly knowledgeable when it comes to tough cases. And as you'll remember from the issues discussed in Chapter One, an awful lot of cases are tough indeed.

To get a glimpse of the level of knowledge out there, I recently surveyed a couple dozen Advanced Book Exchange sellers who were offering low-price U.S. "first editions" of John le Carré's 1962 debut novel, *Call for the Dead*. Since the true first is comparatively scarce, I suspected that all the copies were actually of the far-more-common club edition, which states "first edition" on the copyright page but has several other indications of being a BCE: a different dust-jacket design, no price on the jacket flap, and a blind stamp. And with a quick clarification question, that's what I found—they were all BCEs.

Now, any seller who did a quick informational Web search or checked a price guide or even guessed based on the missing flap price would have immediately seen it as a BCE. But in each case, the seller either hadn't looked closely or, more insidiously, knew the copy was a BCE and listed it as a first anyway, evidently hoping that the buyer wouldn't know better.

The lesson is to do your homework when it comes to apparent bargains. It's far better to ask questions before a sale, or before an auction closes, than to regularly send back items that don't quite meet your standards. Not only will sellers find it annoying and time-consuming, but you'll soon tire of rewrapping books and taking them to the post office, not to mention picking e-mail fights about shipping costs.

**Online auction sites**—at this time, dominated by eBay—best approximate the impulse-buying fun of bookstores. With just a few mouse clicks, you can scroll through hundreds or even thousands of titles, in whichever subjects you're interested in, at your own pace. In short, you're able to genuinely *browse*. Sure, you're spending the time staring at a computer screen, but at least you can sit down and don't have to hold your head sideways to read book spines.

In less than a decade, eBay has grown from an idea to the Internet's most popular destination. Every day, office workers and homebodies, seniors and teenagers, across the nation—and, increasingly, around the world—browse for just about everything, used and new. Literally millions of people have become addicts, spawning several dozen guides to eBay, covering every aspect of buying and selling, from setting up a small business to bidding strategically to taking and posting effective photographs.

As a buyer, the best thing about eBay is that thousands of fresh books appear daily—the equivalent of a massive "New Arrivals" shelf—and that the ignorance gap is alive and well.

Since it'd be a full-time job to even skim all of each day's new book listings, where do you start?

Here's how I do it: Every time I learn of a new book I can't live without, I search on an online-store site—usually ABE—to see what the going rate is; if it's really inexpensive, or there's one copy that's clearly a bargain compared to the others, I'll just buy it. If not, I'll search eBay in the "Books" category, entering just enough information so I get all the available listings without too many extraneous ones. For instance, if I'm looking for copies of William Goldman's novel *The Princess Bride*, I'd input *Goldman* and *Princess Bride*.

I keep a series of these eBay searches bookmarked on my Web browser. Most sellers use the default seven-day-auction setting, so I do my searches once a week. That means I miss out on some "Buy It Now" items and some three- and five-day auctions. But you *have* to draw a line as to how much time you'll be sitting in front of a computer.

The potential problems that you run across shopping on a retail site like ABE are magnified greatly when it comes to online auction sites, especially because the sites themselves assume no responsibility for the items' quality. Most sellers—and certainly the vast majority of those you're interested in—are amateurs, and questions of condition and edition are key. People describe their books as "real nice" or "in OK shape" or "pretty good for a book that is 50 years old!!!" What do you do with *that*? If the price is low enough, you may decide to take your chances; otherwise, go ahead and ask the seller to clarify—as early as possible, to give the seller time to check the book and reply. You're doing a favor for the whole online-auction community: Next time the seller puts up a book for sale, she's likely to include more details, to pre-empt questions such as yours.

With regard to edition: Many sellers don't look to see whether a book is a first; just as many go ahead and assume theirs is a first without even knowing how to make sure. If *you're* not sure from the description and photos, ask questions.

On eBay and other auction sites, shipping costs continue to be a wild card. While fixed-price sites such as ABE have (thankfully) standardized shipping costs, auction sites have not. The result is that, for a particular book, one auctioner's item description may quote a $1.84 media-mail cost; another may state that the "non-negotiable" cost will be $8; another will make no reference at all, leaving it entirely up in the air. Sure, we're talking about only a few bucks, but if you're buying inexpensive books, that can instantly double your cost. If it will make a difference, it's another thing worth asking about before the auction closes.

Every online bidder develops his own personal set of guidelines, and you'll do the same. For instance, I almost never bid on items with reserve prices—I find it a waste of time. But you may disagree. And I generally place bids as close as possible to the auction's close, to protect myself against . . . myself. If another buyer places a higher bid, my impulse is to place a second, higher bid.

It's only natural. People's behavior in auction situations is well-documented: Upon being outbid, they immediately raise their original maximum—after all, if someone is willing to bid $10 more, the item *must* be truly worth that much!

**Nonprofit sales**—most commonly, library or church sales—are great for just about every kind of book, if you find real-time competition more exciting than exhausting.

Library sales are run by a group of volunteers, typically dubbed "Friends of the Library." Though free public libraries are supposed to be taxpayer-supported, decades of shrinking budgets have starved them, and that's where the Friends come in: They work to add books to the circulating stacks and, even more so, to raise funds for operating expenses and acquisitions. A big annual sale can produce tens of thousands of dollars in revenue.

Sales vary widely in quality, from a single rack of discarded, taped-over hardcovers to tens of thousands of individually priced volumes in every conceivable subject area. The best sales are those with a large, broad selection, low prices, and a high percentage of donated—as opposed to discarded—books. The most frustrating are those that try to maximize revenue by slapping a high price on every attractive volume.

Some sales solicit donations; others simply become known as good places to donate. The people who stock up on copies at a particularly rewarding library sale often will return the books when they're done, along with others, to put them back into circulation.

The biggest sales draw serious crowds, particularly right at the beginning, when dues-paying members are allowed in ahead of everyone else. Ambitious dealers and scouts pay to become members of a number of regional Friends support groups. If you're going to go to a sale, it's almost always worth it to pay the entry fee—usually $5 to $20—since dealers, scouts, and other collectors will sniff out most of the obvious gems within the first hour.

And even if you don't come home with a box of astonishing bargains, you'll almost certainly get your money's worth in entertainment, experience, and even exercise. It can be exhilarating to be hunting through boxes and shelves at top speed, hoping that the guy next to you isn't looking for the exact same titles.

On the final day, many sales make a valiant effort to clear out as many leftover volumes as possible by offering amazing deals: $5 a bag, $10 a box, $3 a bag, whatever it takes. True, you probably won't uncover any $150 items, but you can fill in gaps in your hypermodern collection—particularly in the area of dust jackets. If you've bought an autographed first of some 1960s or 1970s novel with a torn DJ or no DJ at all, keep it in mind—you may very well run across a later printing with a serviceable jacket. For plenty of hardcovers, the first-edition jacket is identical to, say, the third—and even if a few points (typically, blurbs or price) differ a bit, isn't it worth 50 cents or a dollar to make your naked copy more attractive? Also, there's no better place to snap up reading copies of books recommended by friends or relatives.

There's a helpful website (www.booksalefinder.com) that lists upcoming and ongoing library sales in your area; it's particularly useful in locating sales near places where you'll be vacationing. Just make sure that when you vanish from your rented lakeside cabin for an afternoon of book shopping, you remember to leave room in the back seat for the kids to sit on the way back home. The website doesn't list everything—it's based on self-reporting—so it's worth a telephone run-through of each branch in your region that's *not* listed, just to make sure.

**Book fairs** offer the opportunity to see truly scarce and desirable items in person and, as important for the ambitious collector, to chat with store owners, dealers, and fellow bibliophiles. Some fairs are smallish, one-day affairs, with no more than a couple dozen regional sellers and a two-dollar admission fee; others feature hundreds of dealers with an enormous range of merchandise. All put you in contact with books and people you wouldn't otherwise see.

What's offered at book fairs is far higher-end than at most bookstores, and you won't find many real bargains. Should you be looking to buy anything at all? Sure. With a collecting focus, you're hunting for titles and themes that few others are, meaning you may find items worth more to you than to their sellers. But your mind-set should encompass gathering information and making contacts as well as buying books—that way you'll feel satisfied even if you leave the convention center empty-handed.

Bookseller Phil Arundel describes fairs as heady experiences for novices. "People getting started in this hobby need to take a deep breath," he says. "When I went to my first book fair, in college, I spent five grand—I thought there would *never be another book.*"

Some book fairs are listed on the www.booksalefinder. com site; others can be found at www.bookfairs.com and www.bookhunterpress.com/index.cgi/bkfairs.html. And as with library sales, it's imperative that you get there at the opening—a lot of prizes disappear quickly, and there's no benefit to waiting.

**Yard sales** are more hit-and-miss than any other book-shopping venue. On a lovely Saturday morning, you may stop at half a dozen sales without finding more than a row of dog-eared Dean Koontz paperbacks. True, if the seller is a real book lover, he's hardly going to set out a box of Faulkner firsts for 50 cents each. But still, it's worth checking: You just might find a stack of cool vintage pocketbooks or old volumes of literary criticism from a long-ago college course.

Moving sales are more promising—after all, books are heavy, and people are looking to get rid of those they can live without. And estate sales are the best bet of all, since the aim is to clear out a deceased person's belongings altogether. Owners tend to sell books in lots rather than individually, so you may find yourself facing the possibility of lugging home much more than you intended. Only you can determine whether it'll be worth the time of sorting and disposing once the boxes are in your garage.

Somewhat surprisingly, wealthy neighborhoods don't necessarily produce the best yard sales—not to mention that the houses are farther apart, so it's less convenient to hop from one to another. College towns, with their high turnover and education levels, are a much better bet. Find out which neighborhood the professors tend to live in, and drive around on a few summer Saturdays. Many cities make things easier by holding annual town-wide yard-sale days, which offer a great opportunity to stroll around new areas and hunt for treasure.

**Flea markets**—good ones, anyway—are basically a compilation of yard sales, all in one place, and so are certainly more efficient than driving from neighborhood to neighborhood, following cryptic, hand-lettered signs posted on lampposts. Ideally, you'll find a number of people with interesting books—possibly next to a pair of old shoes and broken juicer—that they're hoping to not have to lug back home. Some dealers set up shop at flea markets, and as a buyer you'll have to switch gears: As with a bookstore, check a few prices, and if they're too high, move on.

The biggest problem I've found with flea markets is that once you're in book-searching mode, with eyes scanning at ground level for promising-looking boxes, you stop seeing much of what sellers have to offer that *isn't* book-related.

**Auctions** can be intimidating, even in theory. They attract a far higher level of buyer than other venues, and they're far more public—on eBay, when you end up overpaying for a book, almost no one notices, much less snickers. And since attendees—whether in person or not—have had time to study up on what's available, and since they're always on the lookout for bargains they can resell at a profit, the ignorance gap is almost nonexistent.

Where auctions can be invaluable is for collections of very particular types of books that rarely appear for sale and aren't on every other collector's radar screen. If you're accumulating, say, a certain series of 1940s pamphlets, or 1920s cookbooks, or vintage paperbacks featuring a certain painter's cover art, and someone's personal collection of that same focus comes up at auction, you may never have a better opportunity to get so much good stuff at once.

The important thing, then, if you make a practice of checking out auctions: Do your homework, and—just as with online auctions—don't get caught up in bidding and pledge more than you'd planned to spend. Just because a rival is willing to bid more doesn't automatically mean the item is worth more to you.

**Thrift stores** can be fun to roam through (though plenty are depressing as well), and sometimes you'll find one with a large book section. The chances are pretty slim that any spectacular collectibles will show up, but it's always worth a quick scan. What you *can* find are terrific reading copies and the occasional nice first edition from the 1970s or 1980s.

Some thrift stores price books individually (which drastically reduces the chances of landing hardcover bargains). Stores with somewhat upscale merchandise and clientele usually use unobtrusive stickers on the dust jackets, but downscale stores often take much less care with pricing: I've seen everything from heavy black grease pencil on the front flap to price tags stapled (!) to the dust jackets.

**Antique shops** are, I've found, basically useless when it comes to book collecting. Sellers seem to price books based on aesthetics—would this look good on a mantelpiece?—rather than on market value. And even as props, they're generally overpriced for their condition. It's rare that antique dealers, however expert in furniture and glassware and memorabilia, are equally knowledgeable about books. If a volume is old and takes up a lot of shelf space, it'll be marked high. On the off chance that a deceptively low-key modern collectible shows up, it'll likely be in mediocre condition.

The bottom line: If you enjoy wandering into antique stores anyway, walk by the shelf of books, just in case—but keep your expectations low.

## You Can't *Keep* Everything: Strategies for Selling

It might not take long before you realize: *I have a lot of books*. Don't even try to keep every one: You'll run out of shelves, you'll have trouble locating specific books when you want them, and the presence of mediocre copies will downgrade your entire collection—less in terms of value than in overall *feel*. It's important to get into a routine of "deaccessioning": If you don't think you're going to end up keeping a book permanently in your collection, get rid of it, sooner rather than later.

Cull out copies where you easily can: when you've acquired an earlier printing, or a copy in better condition, or one that makes yours obsolete. If you're continually upgrading, you simply can't stay emotionally attached to every copy. Learn how to let go, with no regrets.

When you buy a book on eBay and find that, upon arrival, it's not as cool in person as it looked onscreen, let it go—even if you can't sell it for more than two or three dollars. If the book isn't worth keeping, it doesn't matter that you can't make money selling it.

You'll need to set up a system, formal or informal, of getting rid of books. Before the Internet, it was far easier to pick up good-looking books and take them to the local bookshop to resell them for an easy profit. Now you have to *think* about it. The upside: You have far more control, and your books can bring you far more money.

You want to get the most you can for your books, of course, but without going overboard in trying to squeeze out the last available dollar. Life is too short and your time too valuable.

### The Profit Motive

If you've purchased this book with the express intent to begin a life as a dealer, feel free to skip this brief section. If that *isn't* your intention, pay attention: I want to strongly discourage your taking the step of becoming a professional or semipro book scout, or even thinking primarily in terms of buying books to resell.

Scouts make a living buying books cheap and reselling them quickly. At library sales, they're the ones aggressively elbowing the elderly volunteers out of the way while scooping up armloads of nice-condition paperbacks and trying to psych each other out with loud running monologues about how there's nothing good to be found. (In my library-sale region, one of these guys evidently never bathes, which only adds to his appeal.) Many are perfectly nice people—just not when bargains are at hand.

Of course, dealers and scouts are absolutely essential to the world of collecting books: They're the means by which books are distributed in the first place, to buyers everywhere, in stores and online. And getting rare finds into the hands of dealers means that more collectors can potentially access them—after all, dealers are the ones with access.

But *you* don't need to be one of them. The hobby has plenty of middlemen, and more people scouting for profit means fewer bargains and interesting finds for collectors at the original point of sale. Two even better reasons:

- Nothing sucks the fun out of book collecting like looking at it as a business; and

- Making real money in the hobby requires a tremendous commitment of time and energy. It's not as easy as it was before the Internet brought down the prices of easy-to-find modern first editions.

The situation with regard to both of these points is changing lately. Technology is making it easier to scout, as wireless Internet devices and services like ScoutPal allow scouts to check an item's resale value almost instantly. But taking the guesswork out of it makes it even *less* like a game; it relegates the scout to the role of unskilled labor, scanning bar codes and staring at tiny LCD screens.

Now, all this is not to say that you should pass up a $1 book if you're pretty sure you can resell it for $10 or $20 or more. It's nice to supplement your income and defray the cost of buying more books. I'm saying only that thinking about books' resale value shouldn't be your first priority.

There's even a moral case against buying to resell: Back in 1761, French book-lover Louis Bollioud-Mermet denounced those who "take advantage of the ignorance or the necessities of the seller in the mercenary hope of afterwards finding an unskilled or too eager purchaser. . . . What was once a means of mental culture thus becomes a commodity to gratify their avarice." Ouch.

OK, all of you planning to open your own online bookshops and quit your day jobs—you can start reading again.

**An online store**—setting up shop on ABE, Alibris, or another bookselling site—is potentially the most lucrative option. It's also far and away the most involved and time-consuming.

It'd be inconceivable to open an actual brick-and-mortar bookstore without an inventory of thousands of books, not to mention thousands of dollars. By contrast, anyone can set up shop on the Internet. As Stephen Windwalker writes in *Selling Used Books Online*, "[T]he advent of online used bookselling has greatly lowered the stakes involved in failing as a used bookseller. Instead of losing anywhere from $20,000 to $100,000 and having to hire a lawyer to negotiate one's way out of a multi-year lease and a mountain of publisher and distributor debt, a failed online used bookseller might lose $500 and a lot of time and effort." (This assumes that you intend to open an online bookstore as a profit-making venture rather than as an efficient way to cull extra and unwanted books from your collection.)

An online store is a great way to sell collectible books in better-than-average condition, if you have at least a hundred to sell and the time and energy to handle multiple orders at once. And it's getting easier all the time—you have a lot of choices where to set up shop. (No need to put together an attractive site of your own from scratch.) A particularly helpful website, www.onlinebookselling. net, provides information on each major venue for selling online—from Amazon and ABE to BookAvenue and TomFolio. You'll learn how to upload item descriptions, revise prices, deal with payment options, and everything else you'll need.

Again, buyers' biggest concerns with shopping for books online are condition and edition, so take that into account. Do your best to determine a book's proper edition, and list all the relevant information you can with regard to copyright and points. Be honest regarding condition, and use the terms that are standard within the book-collecting world. A books isn't "nice" or "great"— or, rather, it can be, but separate from its being "very good" or "near fine." Even if a particular defect hardly seems like a defect to you—say, if the dust jacket has been price-clipped, or if the pages are lightly foxed— mention it in your description. You may not care, but the buyer probably will. You don't want the hassle of dealing with returns and refunds, not to mention hostile e-mails.

To paraphrase a cliché, treat buyers and potential buyers as you'd like to be treated.

**Fixed-price sites** such as Amazon Marketplace couldn't make selling books much easier: You just type in a book's title or ISBN, gauge the condition, and come up with a price. The process works best for newish books in near-new condition.

The problem with selling collectible editions—at least as the sites tend to be set up—is that the focus is on low prices. If you're selling an autographed copy of a book, and half a dozen people have the same book unsigned, few buyers will ever see yours—they'll simply grab the lowest-priced one. On Amazon, you can label a book "collectible" only if you're selling it for more than the cover price, which often doesn't make sense. (If you go with Amazon, it's worth investing in Windwalker's *Selling Used Books Online*, which explores that site in great detail.)

On a fixed-price site—and even on a regular online store—you'll want to check back periodically to keep tabs on competing sellers and revise your prices downward accordingly. And you'll want to decide on a price floor: How low is it worth going? Eight dollars? Five dollars? Three dollars? Seventy-five cents?

How long will it take you to evaluate a book's condition, type in the ISBN, check other sellers' prices, input the price—and then, once a sale is made, locate the book and the right size envelope, wrap it up, and take it to the post office? Is all that worth the 75 cents (minus commission, mind you)? Three dollars? Five dollars? Pick a level, and below that, a book should automatically go in a box to take to a bookstore—or to donate.

**An online auction site** such as eBay is the best place to sell books in high current demand—say, a first of the just-announced Pulitzer novel—or that are unusual and hard to find. Best of all are rare books that browsers didn't even know they were looking for: odd travel books, old novels with inflammatory subjects, historical biographies with unusual slants, 1940s pocketbooks with scandalous cover art.

Where you're unlikely to make more than a nominal return—no matter how provocative your item description—is with common books: recent pocketbooks, Oprah club picks four months after their best-seller-list peak, most mystery hardcovers, outdated 1970s nonfiction. These clutter up auction sites and really should be on fixed-price sites instead. If the price runs uncomfortably low there, cut your losses and put the book in the donate box.

If you frequent auction sites as a buyer, you already have a good sense of what browsers are looking for in a subject line, description, and photograph. But it's also important to abide by the information and strict grading guidelines of dedicated bookselling sites—otherwise serious collectors will likely pass your items by.

Want more advice? Pick up one of the dozens—*dozens*—of books with detailed information on selling effectively on auction sites. Or just wing it: eBay and other auction sites keep making it easier to set up and sell. Even dealing with payments now requires little more than a few mouse clicks—though with each innovation, the price of convenience rises.

**Bookstores** are the easiest place to sell your extras. After a while in the hobby, you'll almost certainly find yourself with books you can't use: copies that you forgot you already own, unwanted books purchased in lots with those you *had* to have, books that looked better onscreen than in person, books bought in pursuit of a collecting focus that you later decided to shift. And bookstores are ideal places to take the nice ones.

Store owners depend on people bringing in stock, and most will pay decently for items that they know their customers will buy fairly quickly. That depends, of course, on what the customers want, which is why it's best to check out the store ahead of time, to get a basic sense of what's there and what's not. Chat with the manager—if he has no luck selling, say, science fiction, there's no point in bringing in a box of sci-fi paperbacks. If the clientele snaps up World War II titles, that's the store to take those books to.

Making real money selling to bookstores requires serious effort: familiarizing yourself with individual stores' stock and needs, and taking different sets of books to different stores. Even if you're just trying to dump your extras, it's worth asking some questions—otherwise you're likely to return home with most of what you were hoping to sell.

What *don't* bookstores want to see you bring in?

"Anything by Danielle Steel," says Carey G. Spain of Montclair Book Center in Montclair, New Jersey. "*The Bridges of Madison County. Jonathan Livingston Seagull.* Used travel guides."

"Any *Reader's Digest* condensed book," says Phil Arundel of Arundel Books in Seattle. "And *The Horse Whisperer*. Not that there's anything wrong with the book—and I'd wager we sell quite a few copies of it—but every third person who comes in with a bag of books has that in it."

"College textbooks," says Joel Dumas of North Country Books in Burlington, Vermont. "Dated political biographies. Books about people who are popular for a short time, like Rush Limbaugh or Martha Stewart or Princess Di."

"Computer books that are five years old: *How to Use Word 1.0,*" says Ken Gloss of Boston's Brattle Book Shop. "And outdated social-science books—the pop sociology and psychology books that go out of date six months after they're published."

"We joke about trying to get rid of every copy of *Iacocca* and Arthur Hailey's *Wheels*," says Eugene Okamoto of

Philadelphia-area Harvest Book Co. "We throw them into the recycling bin, maybe five a day every day for the last dozen years. But we haven't made a dent."

What can you expect for books that a store *does* take? A percentage of the cover price—perhaps 10 percent in cash or 20 percent in trade. (A store that's more selective will likely go higher.) Even when the economy isn't depressed, owners are likely to be far more generous with store credit than with cash. Credit always sounds better—you can be a kid in a candy store!—but keep in mind that it's possible that the store won't have enough books in which you're interested. You can always use *some* credit and take the rest in cash, or save the credit for later.

To get rid of those for which the store can't offer you money or credit—and if you'd rather not lug them somewhere else yourself—ask about a donation program. Many stores have set up ways to send books where they can do good. Moe's Books in Berkeley channels unwanted books to a prison-library charity. Harvest Book Co. created a program titled "Good Books, Better Lives" to donate extra children's books to kids without them. Arundel Books passes extras to area thrift stores.

**Auctions** are ideal only in certain circumstances: namely, when you have a focused, valuable collection that you'd like to sell all at once. If you do, by all means check out the possibilities. Information about auctions, scheduled or not, is available on a variety of bibliophilic websites, including those I've listed in Chapter Four.

**At a yard sale or flea market,** just set 'em neatly in boxes, spines out and readable, and see who stops by. At 50 cents or a dollar apiece, you won't be able to retire early on the proceeds, but you'll be spending a relaxing weekend day outdoors, so who's complaining? Don't bother pricing books individually, unless you have a few brand-new or expensive-looking titles, and don't charge more than a buck per hardcover. More than that, and three-quarters of your potential customers will keep on walking.

How do you end up with books more appropriate to a yard sale than anywhere else? You'd be surprised at how quickly they pile up. If you buy a copy of a book with a nice dust jacket to match with another copy, you're left with an extra. You may buy a library-sale copy that, examined more closely at home, proves to be in crummier condition than you'd thought.

**Donating** books to a fund-raiser—library, school, non-profit, church—is a marvelous way to return books to circulation, to give some novice a crack at them. The only danger is restraining yourself from buying your old copies again when you see them at the sale itself!

While you shouldn't load down the poor volunteers with half a ton of marked-up or water-damaged books, you also shouldn't worry too much about culling out *all* the crummy stuff. If the books don't sell at the sale—and you'd be surprised how few are left after a two-bucks-a-bag day—the organization will certainly have a system for distributing leftovers to other organizations.

**Donating** to a thrift store also gets books back into the world, and generates a bit of revenue. Is there a store you like browsing in? or one nearby that funds a cause that you support—women's health, AIDS patients, a church? Load up the backseat and head there.

Sure, most of the books at thrift stores are crummy, and sure, you may be just adding to that crumminess. That's OK—you genuinely never know what someone will buy. And again, if the shop can't sell a book, even at a low price, the proprietor will give it away to someone else. It'll find a home *somewhere*.

Donating to a school or prison reading program cuts out the middleman and gets books straight to where they can do good. Phone a few neighborhood schools—middle or high school, unless you have a lot of children's books—and ask if they're interested.

Several organizations focus on prison literacy; check out the Prison Book Project (prisonbooks.org), Books Through Bars (www.booksthroughbars.org), or the Books Behind Bars program (www.prisonpenpals.net/booksbehindbars.html).

**Throwing away books** seems the worst of all possible sins, practically violating a commandment. But surely not *every* book deserves to be passed on. As a rule, the only volumes that should be discarded rather than just given away are those that are too damaged to qualify as either collectibles or decent reading copies. Even thrift shops and prison programs would prefer not to sort through, say, water-damaged pocketbooks or marked-up old textbooks or musty Reader's Digest volumes before *they* take the initiative to toss them out. And no one—*no one*—wants old issues of *National Geographic*. Every subscriber saves every copy, since they carry a sense of permanence, but eventually they take up just too much space, or the accumulator dies, and someone is stuck with hundreds of yellow-spined magazines that no one really wants. As I type this, a couple thousand eBay sellers are trying to get rid of their old copies—with little success.

Recycling old books is, obviously, preferable to filling up trash cans and landfills. Different municipalities and companies have different rules; it's worth the few minutes it takes to flip through the Yellow Pages and make a phone call or two to find out the best way to recycle.

## Hypermoderns and Beyond: Collecting Today

After a few months on the store shelf, remarkably few contemporary books are worth even as much as their original cover price. Serious collectors tend to look down on books published within the last decade or so—that is, *hypermodern* books.

It's not that books used to be better, or better made, or in any way more collectible, except that there are too many of any hypermodern to *ever* qualify as rare, and that their prices often seem out of whack. It's hard not to be cynical when a favorable *New York Times* review drives up a new biography's price to silly levels, or when a 1996 debut novel hits three figures. Why? Because those prices will *surely* fall. "The part of the market that has collapsed the most in recent years," says Ken Eastman of Moe's Books in Berkeley, "is in modern first editions, from the '60s forward."

Yet many still command high prices—unreasonably high. The booksellers whom I interviewed unanimously

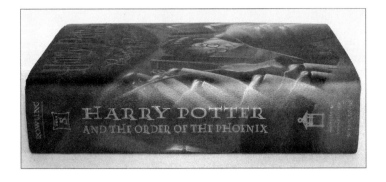

cited hypermoderns when asked to name a category that they felt was overvalued.

**Rare vs. Well-Done.** One of 6.8 million U.S. first editions of J.K. Rowling's latest. Who will pay a premium price for it in twenty years?

So should you refuse to buy anything published after 1990? Of course not. You should just be particularly cautious about how much you spend for them. Once you start looking, you'll find marvelous books of every era—and you'll figure out how to take advantage of the constantly shifting prices that online bookselling creates.

## Rare vs. Well-Done

Are you a Harry Potter fan? Thought so. But are you one of those fans so devoted that they buy two copies of each novel, one to read and one to keep pristine? That may be a smarter move aesthetically than economically: In ten years, just how much will that first edition of *Harry Potter and the Order of the Phoenix* be worth to a collector? After all, Scholastic printed 6.8 million copies to begin with—and that's just the American edition!

Think about it: *6.8 million first editions.* They may be invaluable as sentimental favorites, but there isn't enough demand in the world to balance that supply and make those copies worth anything as collectibles. And considering their widespread critical acclaim and readers' devotion, J.K. Rowling's novels will likely hold their value *better* than other books that have seen massive first printings in recent years.

As a general rule if an author produces a giant best-seller, *her later books will be too plentiful to be collectible.*

That doesn't mean those books aren't worth buying and owning—just that the market value of their first editions will likely never rise as high as their cover price. To name a few ready examples: John Grisham after *The Firm*, Jean M. Auel after *The Clan of the Cave Bear*, Stephen King after *Christine*, Scott Turow after *Presumed Innocent*, Tom Clancy after *The Hunt for Red October*, Dean Koontz after *Twilight Eyes*, Amy Tan after *The Joy Luck Club*. All were published in multiples of hundreds of thousands, or even millions, and are very, very easy to find even in nice-condition first editions.

The Internet's impact on used-book pricing has been felt most dramatically with books such as these. Just about every used bookstore has a Tom Clancy section, and until several years ago, the owner would designate the first-edition copies of *Red Storm Rising* or *Patriot Games* or *The Sum of All Fears* to be collectible and price those at $15 or $20. That's still less than the cover price and doesn't seem like a bad deal. But on the Internet those are now $5 books, and library and yard sales are swamped with them.

For the stores, this poses a real problem: The books take up so much shelf space that it's not economically feasible to charge two or three bucks for a recent Colleen McCullough first edition—not to mention the steady stream of customers bringing in fresh copies to sell, since many fans of these best-selling authors don't feel the need to keep their books after reading them.

There's a double whammy against an author when her books are popular with readers far more than with critics. Some of the authors whose 1980s and 1990s novels aren't worth—and almost surely will never be worth—as much as they cost new: Jeffrey Archer, James Clavell, Jackie Collins, Clive Cussler, Nelson DeMille, Ken Follett, Frederick Forsyth, Andrew M. Greeley, John Jakes, Judith Krantz, Robert Ludlum, Colleen McCullough, James Michener, Lawrence Sanders, Sidney Sheldon, Leon Uris, and Joseph Wambaugh.

### Taking the Prize
By and large, the most collectible authors are those whose works are not only read but critically respected. If an author enters "the canon"—to be kept in print for the foreseeable future, to be taught in high-school English

classes, to be the subject of biographies—her first editions will surely be valuable. There's no question that top-quality books are more likely to be valuable in the long run.

Guides to collecting often list fiction recipients of annual prizes: Nobel Prize, Pulitzer Prize, National Book Award, Booker Prize, PEN/Faulkner award, Edgar, National Book Critics Circle Award, Nebula Award, Whitbread Award, Orange Prize, Newbery Medal, etc. The lists are useful inasmuch as they remind you of award-winners of which you may have been unaware or offer possibilities to look for. But in no way do prizes *guarantee* lasting value.

**Taking the Prize.** *Paco's Story* won the National Book Award, but *Beloved* is, well, beloved.

Years later, prizes aren't seen as infallible indicators of quality—as anyone who watches the annual Academy Awards can attest. (Of course, a National Book Award carries a bit more credibility than an Oscar, but still . . .) Beyond that, there simply aren't enough prizes to go around for all of a given year's significant books, and some aren't discovered till some time after publication. So many great books don't get to put a "Winner!" notice on the paperback edition.

With many books, winning doesn't seem to matter: Toni Morrison's *Beloved* lost the 1987 National Book Award to Larry Heinemann's *Paco's Story*, but today a first of *Beloved* is worth many times more. Anne Tyler's Pulitzer novel *Breathing Lessons* is actually one of her more commonly seen titles and therefore not worth much.

Be careful not to buy during the inevitable price spike that a prize-winner sees immediately after the award ceremony. When the Booker or Pulitzer winner is announced, the value of that book—and of the author's previous books—leaps. A first edition that a week before went for $20 leaps to $150.

And then what happens? The going rate dips a bit, as some people decide they'd rather have $150 than their copies, and then stabilizes. Over the next year or two or five, opinions about the author and book settle, buzz either stays or dissipates, and values shift accordingly. And there are plenty of prize-winning critical favorites that never took off in the collectibles market, such as Alison Lurie's 1984 Pulitzer-winning *Foreign Affairs* and Rafi Zabor's 1997 PEN/Faulkner-winning *The Bear Comes Home*.

Later books by award-winning authors often get no boost at all from the prizes. To cite the most obvious example, Pearl S. Buck won the 1938 Nobel Prize and published some eighty books, but collectors pretty much confine their interest to her 1931 novel *The Good Earth*. And in keeping with general undervaluing of foreign authors, few non-Western Nobel winners carry much value.

The question, then: Do prize-winning books make good investments? In my opinion, not if you buy them soon after the prize is awarded. *Before*, sure—but no one knows which books will win. If you're fortunate enough to be holding a first of the new Pulitzer novel, your best financial move is to sell it on an auction site and then, a year or so later, buy a fresh copy at what will very likely be a drastically reduced price. That is, if it's worth your time and effort—and if you'll remember to buy the book again later. Remember: The goal is to have in your collection great books, not just the memory of them.

## Skyrockets in Flight

Why do some books take off as collectibles while others in exactly the same situation don't? It's all about *buzz*— a factor that, as with so many things about book collecting, is a mystery.

An award isn't necessary—sometimes a front-page write-up in the *New York Times Book Review* is all it takes to set off a mini-frenzy. And it's not only first novels that take off—after all, a dazzling debut seems far less stunning after the author has followed it with two or three works that have left a) no impression on readers or critics and b) extra copies piled in bookshop aisles.

An Oprah Winfrey endorsement produces explosive interest—sometimes among collectors (as with Jane

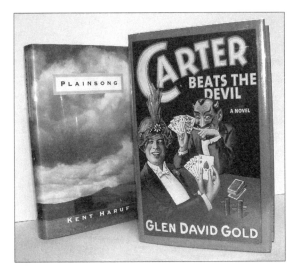

**Skyrockets in Flight.** Great reviews, wide publicity—and too many copies available to maintain high prices.

Hamilton's *The Book of Ruth*), often not (as with Chris Bohjalian's *Midwives*).

The size of a book's first printing—the supply—makes a huge difference in its eventual value. For instance, Kent Haruf's *Plainsong* (1999) and Glen David Gold's *Carter Beats the Devil* (2001), each with a 75,000-copy initial printing, generated bursts of excitement from collectors until they realized that there would be ample supply no matter what the demand. Even autographs and advance reading copies didn't help much in providing collectible versions of the books, since the publishers distributed ARCs widely and both authors signed profusely.

However, whether a breakthrough novel itself develops into a prize collectible, the flash of interest often leads to immediate interest in the author's earlier and usually scarcer books. *Carter Beats the Devil* was Gold's first novel, but *Plainsong* was Haruf's third, and his previous two, neglected and out of print, became hot items overnight.

Some other examples of breakthrough books that made their authors' prior books real collectibles: John Irving's *The World According to Garp*, Kurt Vonnegut's *Slaughterhouse-Five*, Cormac McCarthy's *All the Pretty Horses*,

Oscar Hijuelos's *The Mambo Kings Play Songs of Love*, E. Annie Proulx's *The Shipping News*, Jane Smiley's *A Thousand Acres*, and David Guterson's *Snow Falling on Cedars*. If you happened to own copies of Irving's *The 158-Pound Marriage* or McCarthy's *Blood Meridian* or Smiley's *Barn Blind*, you'd be justifiably pleased. (This is, by itself, a good reason to invest in and hold on to first novels by writers who seem to have potential.)

The pattern isn't universal, though: For whatever reason, other authors' prior work doesn't benefit from the same inflation.

**Gender Trouble.** An advance reading copy of Judith Guest's debut—by all rights a highly collectible book. Alas, no.

Recent Pulitzer winners Peter Taylor, Alison Lurie, Michael Cunningham, Richard Russo, and Michael Chabon saw virtually no bump in collectibility beyond the prize book itself—and sometimes not even that one.

What about *nonfiction* prize-winners and explosive best-sellers? There's usually a bump in the going price, and then a settling. Often there's no premium at all, and you can find the most recent Pulitzer history book on a $5.99 remainder table. Once in a while, a nonfiction book will soar to baffling heights: I'm still waiting for someone to explain to me why signed firsts of David McCullough's 2001 John Adams biography go for $150—and that's down from $250 just a few months ago!

## Gender Trouble

Judith Guest's *Ordinary People* was an unexpected sensation upon its 1976 publication. It was adapted into a hit Hollywood film and remains in print as both a paperback and audio book. Yet the first edition runs only about five dollars. It's not a book that people hold on to, and collectors have responded to the oversupply by driving down the price.

Why? The easiest explanation is that *Ordinary People* falls into the category of women's fiction.

While female authors are well-represented among collectible books, there's undeniably a prejudice against women's fiction, whether critically respectable (Guest) or pure beach reading (Danielle Steel). They're simply not books in which collectors have ever taken a real interest, from the flood of novels that swamped the nation after the Civil War (women wrote nearly three-quarters of the American novels published in 1872) to today's historical romances.

This means that if you run across an early first edition by Belva Plain or Maeve Binchy or Judith Krantz—or Sidney Sheldon, to cite just one male author who writes women's fiction—it's unlikely to carry much value regardless of whether it's in great condition or comparatively scarce. If you're collecting that author, or books of that genre or subject or year, go for it, but don't hope for much on the resale market. Even few of the gorgeously bound domestic novels of a century ago are worth much (again, here's an opportunity!).

Naturally, there are exceptions. There are *always* exceptions: Daphne du Maurier's *Rebecca*, Alice Sebold's *The Lovely Bones*, and others—plenty of them. You'll learn which ones soon enough.

Incidentally, what about actual romance novels—that is, Silhouette, Harlequin, and other paperback and hardcover genre books? They may be highly prized among the notoriously voracious fans of the genre, but only a scant handful (including very early Harlequin romances and a few odd volumes such as Linda Howard's 1998 book *The Mackenzie Family*) are truly collectible.

## Just Not Worth Much

*Encyclopedias*. Sure, they're interesting to flip through. So flip through them, and leave them where you found them. With few exceptions—in particular, the 1911 eleventh edition of the *Encyclopedia Britannica*—they aren't worth anything as collectibles. Plus they take up a tremendous amount of shelf space and cost a relative fortune to ship.

*Books from "library" series*. Those nice old copies of Modern Library books, even with dust jackets, are seldom worth more than a few dollars. And neither is almost any book published under the imprint of a "Home

Library" or "Riverside Library" or something similar. They're not first editions, and the titles are usually ones published under countless different imprints.

*Old textbooks.* Again, more curious than valuable. The exception is with really old books—say, before 1850—that are in unusually good condition. Old textbooks might fit your collecting theme, but don't expect them to take off in value.

**Modern Business Books.** Major impact on our lives; of no interest to collectors.

*Biographies and autobiographies of current pop-culture icons.* You don't need me to point out the transience of most celebrities' fame. But perhaps more important is that a book rushed out to capitalize on its subject's notoriety will surely be published in great quantities—and you know what *that* does to values. As J. Herbert Slater wrote in 1905's *How to Collect Books*, "The celebrity of an author materially affects the value of the book he has written, but nevertheless such book must be difficult to acquire or that value will be small." The same applies to books *about* celebrities.

*Modern business books.* They're almost instantly dated. Books built around the examples of particular successful companies become obsolete when those companies, almost invariably, go bad. (The classic example is Tom Peters and Bob Waterman's 1982 best-seller *In Search of Excellence: Lessons from America's Best-Run Companies*, which profiled a number of companies whose excellence vanished soon after being written about.) Books that predict economic booms or busts are usually proven wrong—and even if they turn out to be prescient, so what? Personal-finance books are disposable. Collectors have no interest in even the uncommon firsts of publishing phenomena such as the insipid *Who Moved My Cheese?*—and I'm not about to advise you to start scouring bookstore shelves for *that*.

*Bibles.* Obviously, a sixteenth- or seventeenth-century Bible is probably worth plenty, and your family Bible may be of tremendous sentimental value. But we're talking

about the book that's been printed far more often, in different editions, than any other work, producing a supply-demand balance that's stacked so heavily toward the supply side that it practically *can't* be worth anything. In fact, surprisingly few religious books have much value to collectors, except for works by significant historical figures or some of particular interest; for instance, I'm fascinated by the colorfully apoplectic anti-Catholic volumes published toward the end of the nineteenth century—and even those are rarely valuable.

**Chapter and Verse.** Many poetry volumes squeeze into a small space.

## Chapter and Verse

If you've never heard of a poet apart from seeing her name on a bookstore shelf, it's unlikely that her books are worth much. Possible, but unlikely. That doesn't mean poetry books aren't worth watching for and buying—in fact, there are plenty of reasons why aspiring collectors might want to go just that direction. I mean only that if you stumble across a cool 1920s volume of poetry at a library sale, or see an eBay listing for an obscure signed book of verse, don't count on having scored a priceless treasure.

Poetry is, traditionally, the least remunerative form of writing; only a scant handful of poets *in the world* make a living by only writing. (Even some truly great twentieth-century poets, like Wallace Stevens and William Carlos Williams, have maintained careers completely outside the creative arts. Stevens worked as an accountant; Williams was a physician.) Comparatively few people read it anymore, even fewer will pay money to own volumes of it, and, as a result, publishers—at least those of the last hundred or so years—have been pretty stingy when it comes to bringing out fresh volumes.

But a great many amateurs feel the need to express themselves through poetry, and the result is thousands of self-published or *very* small-press volumes of verse. Most are genuinely scarce, since only a handful were printed, and many bear the author's signature, since they were either given as gifts or sold at readings. Some of the poetry is perfectly good; most—as you'd expect—is pretty awful.

And less than you might think is collectible, apart from first editions of household-name poets—Eliot, Dickinson, Sexton, Frost, Ginsberg. Look at the last decade's winners of the Pulitzer poetry prize: Philip Levine, Jorie Graham, Lisel Mueller, Charles Wright, Mark Strand, C.K. Williams, Stephen Dunn, Carl Dennis, and Paul Muldoon. First editions of nearly all of their prize-winning books can be had for less than $20—barely more than their original list price—even though the print runs were comparatively small.

I don't want to overstate this point. First editions of *earlier* works by these poets can be quite valuable, and there is indeed a thriving high-end poetry market, as evidenced by the continuing success of a number of specialist dealers. It's undeniably worth familiarizing yourself with the genre's high spots and looking up items as you come across them. But just as certain is the fact that there *isn't* a market for the vast majority of poetry titles.

That very factor gives the verse enthusiast a good reason to take on just that collecting focus—less competition, and the opportunity to compile a library that's unusual and even unique. There's another, very practical reason: Except for career-summary anthologies, poetry books are slim, meaning that you can fit three or four times as many volumes into the same shelf space.

## Uncollectible—or Undercollected?

If you're working toward a collection of a particular type or genre, you shouldn't pass up an old book just because it wouldn't go for four figures at a Sotheby's auction. Here are a few types of books that seem as though they should be more valuable than they are—and they may be, if building a great personal library matters more than investment value.

*Old travel books.* Surely these must be worth *something*, right? Well, some of them are. But there are an awful lot of turn-of-the-century volumes with titles like *Travels in the Holy Land* or *Voyage to Africa*, written by American or European pilgrims or tourists, and they're prettier than they are collectible. Arguably, these books are undervalued, being both of historical interest (if not significance) and often quite attractive, and therefore an opportunity. Just be careful—before buying a book or placing a bid, check the price of comparable volumes.

*Books by important businesspeople.* Nowadays, every corporate vice president of marketing spits out a lesson-filled memoir, destined for obsolescence a week or two after its publication. But many great industrialists and business thinkers have also produced books about their lives and ideas, and considering the enormous impact these men had and continue to have on millions of working people, the volumes are arguably wildly undervalued—even autographed. You can pick up books signed by the likes of Alfred P. Sloan of General Motors or Thomas Watson of IBM for, comparatively, peanuts. Those by important theorists such as Peter Drucker and W. Edwards Deming are worth even less.

*Old etiquette books, "compendiums of knowledge," and books about sex.* It's not hard to find attractive, curious volumes from the 1880s or 1890s that compile available information on then-useful topics. They sometimes have

**Memoirs of Political Figures.** Worth far less than they should be.

great titles, fascinating photos, and hilariously dated advice. They're also so common as genres that they're rarely of much value. There's a wide opening here: You could build a terrifically provocative library of old books on sex (including advice-to-teens tracts and happy-marriage guides) alone.

*Memoirs of political figures.* Upon retirement—and maybe even before—just about every congressional aide, postmaster general, and White House press secretary writes a book. Few are worth reading, and even fewer are worth collecting, unless your interest is in collecting everything relating to, say, a particular presidential administration, or to everything on politicians from Oklahoma. This meager valuation seems justifiable—except when it comes to elected officials of national stature. Even autographed books by governors or U.S. senators of fifty or a hundred years ago command almost nothing on the rare-book market. These were people who, at the time, were among the nation's most politically powerful figures, but they're generally forgotten today—unfortunately unsurprising in this apolitical, apathetic nation.

Apart from U.S. presidents, a handful of famous secretaries of state (John Foster Dulles, Henry Kissinger, Colin Powell), and a few governors, politicians simply aren't good collectible authors. The occasional celebrity politician (John McCain, Rudolph Giuliani, Hillary Clinton) may draw a brief flash of collector enthusiasm, but it's almost certain to dissipate, sooner rather than later. As for the losing candidate in a presidential election, forget about it: Books signed by Wendell Willkie, Adlai Stevenson, Eugene McCarthy, and Bob Dole are worth so little that it's easy to forget that each of these men had millions of volunteers who put time and money behind their campaigns—not to mention the tens of millions of Americans who cast votes for them.

Keep this in mind before splurging on books by politicians. After all, if we don't remember or care about our governors and senators a decade or two after they've left office, what makes you think we'll care about the recently departed secretary of transportation in 2030?

It's worth pointing out once again that the comparatively low value of all these books is no reason not to collect them—indeed, it may well be a reason to actively seek them out. How about a collection of books by every losing presidential candidate? Hmmm . . .

## Condition Is Everything—Almost

Books with dust jackets get two grades—the first for the book, second for the jacket. That's why you'll see descriptions like NF/VG, which means that while the book is near fine, the jacket shows some wear.

With some slight variations, the levels of condition are:

**Very Fine**
As new, without even the defects that a new book may come with, such as a slightly off-center dust jacket or folded-over corner.

**Fine**
Almost pristine, with allowances only for age—an eighty-year-old book simply cannot look as fresh-off-the-new-releases-shelf as a five-year-old book.

## Near Fine

The most appropriate level for most almost-perfect books. A tiny bit of crumpling to the top of the spine, very slight bumping to a corner or two, the jacket flap price-clipped, a previous owner's neat signature on the end-paper—any of these will bump a book's condition down to NF. Any defect that doesn't fall under the heading of "shelfwear" should be specified.

## Very Good

A copy with two or more of these defects, and/or dust-jacket wear, from light rubbing and sunning to short tears and small nicks. Bibliophiles add + and − to VG to further delineate the magnitude of the defects. Hardcore collectors pretty much ignore modern-era books below VG+, even if they look perfectly nice under a plastic jacket protector.

## Good

Complete but with defects that are quickly apparent: fragile binding, heavily rubbed or chipped jacket, water stains, noticeably bumped corners, faded jacket or spine. Usable as a placeholder copy. An ex-library copy doesn't really get any better than G+.

## Fair

Complete but that's about it. You wouldn't want a *fair* copy on your shelves.

## Poor

Don't even bother. An incomplete copy or one that has been, to use a technical term, trashed.

Apart from vintage automobiles and musical instruments, books are close to the most complex objects that one could choose to collect. Stamps, coins, baseball cards, LPs, Ming vases, even comic books—other collectibles have fewer elements and, therefore, fewer things that can go wrong.

Five "very good" copies of the same book may look quite different, featuring one or more of dozens of possible defects, in varying degrees. Think of all of the pieces: front cover, back cover, joints and hinges, spine, glue, binding, endpapers, flaps, and corners, plus hundreds of pages.

It's an awful lot to keep pristine. And books are meant to be read, displayed . . . *handled*. They're pretty sturdy when it comes to staying readable, but collectors have much higher standards than readability.

Those varying standards are the single biggest differentiator between the reader and the collector. "Many people believe that if a book is twenty or thirty years old, it is in very good condition if the covers are still attached," write Allen and Patricia Ahearn in *Book Collecting 2000*. First-time eBay sellers will refer to a book as being "in great condition" when any collector would see bumps, tears, and fading at first glance.

Other collectibles have many more quality grades—for sports cards (slips of cardboard!), Beckett has invented an elaborate scale that involves a strict 1-10 grade for each of four categories—but none has such variability, or such a broad and colorful dictionary of terms to describe each defect ("What's *foxing* again?" my wife asks). Books can have *toning* or *cracked hinges* or *shelfwear*; they can be *bumped* or *sunned* or *shaken*. See the glossary in back for definitions of these and more.

Not only can a book suffer each of these indignities—each can exist in varying degrees: *slightly bumped, heavily sunned, badly shaken*. You can see why grading a book carries some degree of subjectivity—and why one VG+/VG copy isn't necessarily an upgrade from a VG/VG− copy. It's important, therefore, for sellers to always specify any defects at all.

This pickiness is nothing new, particularly on these shores. Writing a century ago, English author W. Carew Hazlitt offered a bemused take on condition: "The American collector grows more fastidious every day, and discovers blemishes which we on this side of the water try to tolerate, if the article is rare or we badly want it. Our Transatlantic friends . . . go so far as to return purchases not answering the description in the auctioneer's catalogue to their English commission-agents."

And in the last two decades, says Boston bookseller Ken Gloss, collectors have come to value *very fine* books to an unprecedented degree. "The perfect copy," he says, "now goes for *much* more than copies with any defect at all."

## Standards High and Low

The standard advice—and it's perfectly good—is to buy the best-condition book you can afford. Doing that means that you'll never have to upgrade based on condition. But this is important too: Don't let an obsession with condition spoil the fun of collecting. Browsing at library sales and hole-in-the-wall bookshops means looking through stacks of books with dings and tears, and if you limit yourself to mint-condition copies, you'll go home empty-handed.

It's tempting to take advantage of other collectors' finickiness, to say that if certain elements—for instance, remainder marks—don't matter to you, then don't worry about them. Since serious collectors will pay a bit extra for a book whose dust jacket is not price-clipped, you can save money by lowering your standards a hair. And on your shelf at home, it'll look exactly the same whether the jacket is clipped or not.

But consider this: If and when you do decide to sell off some of your collection—and again, I highly recommend periodically culling out books to make space and defray costs of acquiring new items—you won't make back what they're worth unless they're in top condition, and that means the little stuff, like remainder marks and price-clipping. Also, you may change your standards eventually about the grade of books that you want in your collection. It's something to consider when deciding whether to spend the extra five bucks for a VF copy rather than a VG+ copy. I've bought any number of books over the years that looked OK at the time but have since given way to better-condition copies—overall, a wasteful and redundant process.

And you should think twice—or more—when considering books graded good or less. In *Modern Book Collecting*, Robert A. Wilson recommends *never* acquiring copies with blatant defects: for instance, missing pages. "You will always have an incomplete copy, one that will be difficult if not impossible to resell, and one that is of little interest to anyone," he writes. "And you yourself will always want a better, perfect copy."

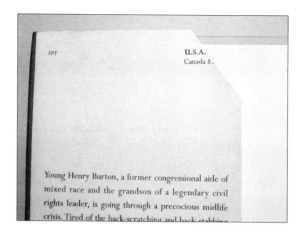

**How Much
Does It Matter?**
Books with
price-clipped
DJs are *always*
less desirable.

## How Much Does It Matter?

A sizable percentage of books carry small defects introduced after their actual publication: price-clipped dust jackets, bookplates, ownership stamps, prior-owner signatures, remainder marks. Unfortunately, these do impact a book's value—and nearly always in a negative way.

I've never understood why people clip the prices off dust jackets before bestowing the books as gifts, as though it's a secret how much a book sells for. But early on, it became common practice, and a huge percentage of books from the 1950s through the 1980s are clipped. It's less common now, though no more rational. What this means is that DJs that are *not* clipped command a small premium—tiny in the case of books that aren't particularly collectible, larger for older books usually found without DJs at all.

Bookplates also seem to be less common than they once were. Unless the previous owner was either famous or somehow connected to the author—making the book an *association copy*, about which I'll write more in the next chapter—the presence of a bookplate reduces a book's value. The extent to which it does depends on a host of variables: the plate's size, prominence, condition (complete is better than torn off), and how much difference it makes to the collector. Likewise, ownership stamps are considered minor defacements. A few bookstores routinely—and, in my opinion, inexcusably—deface their own books by stamping the store logo along the edges or on the end flap.

Prior-owner signatures and inscriptions can be far more serious: Some people write their names neatly, concisely, and as unobtrusively as possible, in ballpoint on the inside of the front board; others scrawl in Sharpie across the whole endpaper. Again, if the ownership signature marks the book as an association copy, then it's an asset, not a detriment. Also, in the case of antiquarian books, some collectors don't mind an unusually attractive signature, especially when the owner has dated the book as well.

Remainder marks vary widely. Added by either the publisher or a discounter, a mark indicates that a book is being sold new at a reduced price, after failing to sell out its print run at full price. (I'll discuss remainders in more detail next chapter.) Sometimes the mark is a minuscule dot at the bottom of the block of pages; other times it's a broad red stripe across the top. A few publishers use an attractive stamp of the company logo.

Obviously, the neater, smaller, and less obtrusive a remainder mark is, the better. With some books—particularly those that were completely unappreciated upon their initial publication and sold hardly anything—it's hard to find copies *without* marks. In these cases, there's a measurable premium for unmarked books.

### A More Perfect Union

A dust jacket without a book is, obviously, of little use to a reader. But to a collector, a book without a jacket is often of even less use. Indeed, a DJ frequently carries far more value than the book that it's intended to protect, being both scarcer and more fragile.

So what should you do when you end up with a jacketless book?

If I end up with a book lacking the jacket—typically, an autographed 1940s or 1950s title—the first thing I do is check online stores to see how much it would cost to get a plain copy with a decent DJ. If it's cheap, I'll usually go ahead and do it.

But you should think twice before following my lead. Marrying dust jackets and books that didn't start out together "is frowned upon by serious collectors," writes Ian Ellis. "Again, the whole mythos behind the first edition is to get a copy of the book in as close to its original state as possible. *Any* alterations detract from this." His advice: "Use your own moral judgment on whether or not to replace, but be aware that it's not an entirely kosher thing to do."

In my opinion, that's a bit harsh—it implies that any defect to the jacket basically destroys the book it's protecting as well. Few of us can afford a standard so high. Even the stern Robert Wilson agrees: "I see no harm in [marrying] as long as the correct jacket is placed on the book and the binding of the book itself is not worn or faded."

If you *do* decide to occasionally buy a DJ to match a book (or vice versa), be careful: The different editions of many books mean that they may not even *fit* together, much less match in a collectible sense. This is particularly true when it comes to books published during wartime, when publishers kept adjusting page size and paper thickness to match supply and restrictions.

For both fit and collectibility, it's important to make an exact pairing. If your book is a fourth printing, you should make an effort to marry it to a jacket from a fourth-printing copy, unless you know for sure that a different printing's jacket is an exact duplicate. Often jackets will carry small codes indicating their printing date, or the cover price may change, or the blurbs on the back cover or inside flap may be updated.

Needless to say, you should never attempt to *sell* a married book and jacket to a serious collector without acknowledging your matchmaking.

## Out of Circulation

As soon as a public library acquires a new book, it modifies it for security and circulation, adding stamps, spine labels, DJ protectors, and/or card pockets. When it discards the book, for whatever reason—lack of shelf space, overstock of a certain title, waning reader interest, a newer edition—those modifications stay with the book.

Library sales, obviously, are the most likely place to find ex-library copies, but plenty find their way to bookshops and online sellers' inventory—where you should avoid them under almost all circumstances. Only ex-library

copies of valuable firsts—say, books that would otherwise be worth several hundred dollars—are worth considering, and even then they're no better than placeholders. At best, you can salvage the dust jacket and hope to locate a cheap first edition lacking its own.

With a good deal of work, an ex-library copy can be made presentable: Stickers can be peeled off, stamps can be (mostly) erased, glue can be removed. But it's still an ex-lib copy. When a for-sale listing uses the phrase "with all usual markings," expect the worst.

**Out of Circulation.** Whether an ex-library book is as extensively marked up as this copy of Alice Walker's *Meridian*, it's still an ex-library copy.

And with some books, you have to be particularly cautious. Academic hardcovers, small-print-run novels, and many children's titles sell more copies to libraries than to the public, meaning that used copies are far more common in ex-lib condition than not.

Books from private circulating libraries are considered ex-lib copies even if they lack the most damaging elements, such as card holders, rebindings, and spine labels. Obviously, their value isn't hurt to the same extent. As with any books, condition is somewhat subjective. Whether you're considering buying or selling an ex-lib copy, use caution and common sense.

### But You Can Still Read It Fine!

When it comes to hypermodern books, collectors expect basically perfect condition. It doesn't seem an unreasonable standard—they're common books, and they haven't been around long enough to endure much aging or shelfwear.

That standard doesn't leave much margin for error. As a collector, you shouldn't settle for copies of 1990s hardcovers with torn dust jackets or gift inscriptions. As a seller, you shouldn't be surprised that no one's interested in buying your (slightly) defective books.

There's no question that this can be aggravating: If an online seller neglects to pad a book before shipping it, and it suffers bumped corners as a result, your new book is worth maybe a third less than it was when it left the dealer's hands. Even more common is a visitor—or even you, in a hurry—pulling a book down from one of your shelves and accidentally tearing the top of the spine. The lesson: Be as careful as you reasonably can.

## Staying in Shape: Keeping Your Books in the Best Condition You Can

Most guides recommend storing books in enclosed, glass-fronted shelves. This is lovely—but somewhat impractical if you own more than a few hundred collectible volumes and don't live in a mansion with a library room as climate-controlled as a refrigerated wine cellar.

The important thing is to minimize damage and deterioration, to maintain books in as close to the original condition as you can. That means keeping them away from sunlight, from moisture, from chocolate-stained fingers, from insects, from carelessly groping browsers, from deteriorating newspaper clippings, from toddlers. In *Modern First Editions*, British author Joseph Connolly grumpily advises collectors "to persuade all babies and animals to live in another [house]—and if you really value your books, only offer hospitality to illiterates who won't persist in bloody touching them all the time."

You don't need barrister bookcases or a child-free home to protect your treasures, but you *do* need to take some precautions.

### First, Do No Harm

Follow the doctor's credo.

- Don't write your name and address on the first page.

- Don't paste in a bookplate.

- Don't use an ownership stamp.

If you're the type of person who likes to lend books to friends, I commend you, being of similar disposition. But you can't trust *anyone* to treat your prize possessions as well as you would—nineteenth-century English essayist Charles Lamb labeled book-borrowers "mutila-

**First, Do No Harm.** Unless you're famous, keep your ownership stamp away from your collectible books.

tors of collections" and "spoilers of the symmetry of shelves"—and under no circumstances should you begin defacing your collection. What's next, card holders and bar codes?

One solution: Make up special bookmarks, or buy some and personalize them, and slip one inside each book that goes home with a friend. It's hardly a perfect system, since you'll still have to keep track of everything you've lent out, need to remind people to return your books, and worry about what shape they'll be in when you finally do get them back. But it's a start.

A better solution—albeit one far more space-consuming—is to purchase paperback copies of favorite books, whenever you find them cheap, and hand them out. If you don't get them back, no problem!

In fact, you may find that two copies of each favorite is insufficient. Nineteenth-century English collector Richard Heber justified his insatiability with impeccable logic: "Why, you see, sir, no man can comfortably do without three copies of a book. One he must have for a show copy, and he will probably keep it at his country-house; another he will require for his own use and reference; and unless he is inclined to part with this, which is very inconvenient, or risk the injury of his best copy, he must needs have a third at the service of his friends."

Yeah—why *not* keep three copies of each book? If only our spouses were more understanding . . .

## Preserved in Plastic

The next step is to begin protecting your dust jackets. A paper jacket is, obviously, a book's most fragile element, vulnerable to something as harmless as a crooked index finger pulling a book off a shelf. If a jacket has tears, under no circumstances should you reach for the cellophane tape. *Tape repairs* only decrease a book's value, and even if you're able to fix a tear so subtly that it's invisible to casual inspection, who knows what that tape will look like in twenty or thirty years?

The solution is plastic jacket covers, which are, fortunately, becoming easier to find and purchase. The best-known manufacturer of covers is Brodart—indeed, the name is sometimes used generically to refer to covers in general—but several companies make them, and you may prefer one over the others. (I've listed a number of them in Chapter Four.)

Covers come in many different sizes, usually measured by the half-inch. Take a ruler and measure some of your books that you think should be protected, to see which sizes are most common, and purchase a smallish number of covers to try them out. Some bookstores helpfully stock sampler packs of jacket protectors. The covers are easy to put on without any kind of tools or equipment, though I recommend purchasing a *bone folder* to help apply creases as needed.

Which jackets need protection? Certainly not all of them. If you own many thousands of books, the task of covering all those jackets is daunting—not to mention that a

**Preserved in Plastic.** *(above left)* Cellophane tape may be transparent now, but check back in a few decades.

**Protecting the DJ.** *(above right)* Installing a plastic jacket protector, using a bone folder.

thousand 25-cent covers cost a total of $250. You'll be able to tell which ones to do. Protect those made from flimsy paper, those suffering from tears, and those that aren't easily and inexpensively replaceable. You can buy pocketbook-size covers as well.

Is it worth protecting older books that don't have jackets? Absolutely—though the process is more laborious: You may have to buy rolls of mylar and cut them to the proper size yourself.

Incidentally, when preparing to carry hardcovers to author signings, you have to choose whether to leave on the dust jackets. Most collectors do leave them on—protected, of course—but I generally leave them at home. Why risk damaging them?

## On the Shelves Themselves

See that the books on your shelves are upright and neat. Bookends are important not only to keep books from falling off the ends of shelves but to ensure that they don't lean against each other. It doesn't take all that long before a book's hinges stretch and it adopts a permanent lean, called *rolling*. No reason to spend a great deal on bookends, unless you want something quirky or elaborate—inexpensive, basic, T-shaped metal bookends are fine. For purposes of preservation, the best way to arrange books is according to their size, since a tall book between two shorter ones will, eventually, splay at the top. (Too bad that this method of arrangement isn't conducive to helping you locate a particular book when you need to.)

Dust is a problem in some houses; if the rims of your vases and top edges of your framed photos collect dirt, you'll need to worry about your books. You can dust soiled books individually by brushing away dirt with a soft cloth. First, though, try the most obvious solution: blowing gently.

Don't shelve books in rooms in which you smoke. You shouldn't be smoking indoors anyway! Fireplace smoke isn't healthy for your books either.

Excessive humidity can be dangerous to your books—at damp times, paper dust jackets may feel soggy, and soft-covers can begin to splay.

Use air-conditioning, a dehumidifier, or even moisture-absorbing crystals such as Dri-Z-Air and DampRid. If your collection includes leatherbound books, *lack* of humidity can also be a problem.

**On the Shelves Themselves.** A victim of humidity.

And then there's sunlight, which fades spines and covers faster than you might think. You've seen how, in video-rental stores and big used bookstores, there's often one shelf near a window that's clearly spent too much time in the sun—all the spines have turned gentle shades of pink and blue.

Nothing this dramatic would happen to your book spines right away, but just in case, try to arrange your bookshelves so they don't fall into the path of sunlight. Or you can always keep the blinds drawn, if you prefer a cavelike living atmosphere. Direct sunlight isn't the only kind that ruins books—indirect sunlight and even bright lamps, given some time, will show effects.

All this gets more than a little frustrating: How on earth can you show off your library if it's in the dark?

As you're probably all too aware, it's not always easy to balance the demands of owning shelves and shelves of books . . . and of keeping up a house.

## The Envelope Solution

I go out of my way to clip reviews and articles from newspapers and magazines relating to a book, its author, or its topic. The most convenient place for this paper—which falls under the category of *ephemera*—is, naturally, in the book itself.

But books don't take well to being packed with paper. Newsprint leaches acid into adjacent pages, leaving unsightly, permanent stains, and more than a few sheets tucked inside a front cover can stretch the binding. The solution is to purchase envelopes that you can slip unobtrusively next to each shelved book, and slip any related paper into them.

**The Envelope Solution.** Do pasted-in clippings make this Andrew Carnegie book less valuable? or more so?

But you may elect not to take that step, for a perfectly justifiable reason: The addition of clippings adds context to a book, in the same way that a prior owner's inscription can. For instance, here's a 1886 first edition of *Triumphant Democracy*, written (and inscribed) by industrialist and philanthropist Andrew Carnegie, that the original owner used as a scrapbook. Every blank page at the front and back of the book is covered with pasted-in newspaper clippings about the author, dating from just after the book's publication to Carnegie's death in 1919.

Officially, this copy should be worth much less than a plain one—the newsprint has stained the adjacent pages, and their presence itself is undesirable—but I'm not so sure. To me, the clippings and provenance, displaying the owner's veneration of Carnegie, give the book *added* value.

In her preface to *The Booklover's Repair Manual*, Estelle Ellis encapsulates this idea, putting the entire idea of book preservation in charming perspective: "Conservation professionals tell us that so-called enclosures, such as book reviews, news clippings, and pressed flowers, break the bindings and leave difficult-to-remove paper stains," she writes. "But what these knowledgeable people see as damaging to a book's health may, for us, enrich the book's value. The trade-off is clear. The choice is yours to make, depending on the place a particular book holds in your life and your expectations for its life span."

Don't get me wrong: Not every book merits this level of affection. For the vast majority of books, envelopes (preferably acid-free ones, since they'll be touching your books) are a good idea. If you love a book so much that you'd like to turn it into a scrapbook, consider buying a second volume and keeping it pristine.

## Can It Be Fixed?

The answer is probably yes: Many of a book's defects can be repaired—if money, time, and effort are no object. But usually they are.

Some remainder marks can be sandpapered off; some stains can be bleached away; torn corners can be professionally restored using swatches of as-close-as-possible matching paper. Steps this drastic are only rarely worth it. None of these should be attempted casually and, probably, not at all.

Many books from different eras are printed with particularly acidic paper, and there's not much you can do about their premature aging. At a signing event several years ago, Susan Sontag remarked to me that none of her books had visibly aged except those published in the late 1960s—on those, the pages were brown and disintegrating.

When is it worth it to take a book to a bindery or professional restorer? When what you're looking at is truly rare and truly valuable—and old enough to be difficult to find in its original binding—then by all means, take it to a bookbinder and ask for a professional opinion. (Note: When an online seller lists a book as a "good candidate for rebinding," it's probably not.)

Here's what you *can* do: You can glue sagging bindings. You can erase pencil and even some pen markings. You can repair some closed dust-jacket tears. You can clean dirty pages and edges. You can mend fraying spine tops.

What do you need to buy? Again, dust-jacket covers. Acid-free glue, such as polyvinyl acetate. A bone folder. Acid-free envelopes. Thin white cotton gloves, if you're handling old, fragile books—or if you have a chocolate habit. A soft brush (bamboo, perhaps) for cleaning dust and eraser remnants. A few erasers of varying softness.

As a marvelous introduction, I recommend Estelle Ellis's *The Booklover's Repair Kit: First Aid for Home Libraries*

(Knopf). It's a bit pricey—$125 list, though you may be able to find it for less online—but comprehensive and arts-and-craftsy. It's also cleverly designed (like an over-size book) and a beautiful item on its own. You have a birthday coming up, don't you?

The *Repair Kit* helps you fix many problems at home, some with simple household materials—but some of its suggested repairs are collecting no-nos. For instance, the authors recommend using tape to fix torn pages and dust jackets, but collectors frown on introducing foreign materials to a book, damaged or not. Always remember that a book is more valuable the closer it is to its original, first-edition state.

## Packing Up

What's the best way to store, move, and ship books? When it comes to storage, dry is better than damp, cool better than hot, dark better than light, clean better than dusty. Attics, therefore, are generally preferable to base-ments; concrete-lined, temperature-stable storage units may be better than either.

Books should be stored standing on end rather than stacked; it's never a good idea to stack books—particu-larly hardcovers—for long. I prefer plastic crates to card-board boxes—they're sturdier and can be much more easily lifted and carried—but their open sides and tops require additional covering, such as a tarp.

For shipping as well as storage, cardboard boxes are the simplest, but they're vulnerable to corners being bumped as well as the other indignities that mail can suffer en route to its destination. The best solution is to use plastic bubble wrap around the edges, particularly at the corners, and to fill in any gaps between books, to pre-vent shifting.

An obvious point but one worth pointing out anyway: If you're storing a lot of books, you likely have too many for your house or apartment. You don't get nearly as much pleasure from books tucked away in an attic as from those on display. So definitely think about sizing your collection to your living space.

Not that I follow my own advice: In my last move—for-tunately, the first in nine years and the last for years to come, I hope—movers lugged some *seven tons* of books from one apartment to another. They were relieved to learn that the destination was on the first floor.

Back in 1862, bibliophile John Hill Burton offered cautionary advice to collectors: "[L]et no man gather together more books than all of us who are tolerably well-to-do have in this country, unless he has good reason to believe himself settled in a home for life. The moving and reshelving of anything like a library—this is, of more than a thousand or twelve hundred volumes—is inexpressibly troublesome and vexatious; and besides, let it be done with as much care as possible, the books are almost sure to receive some injury." ◘

# 3

# THE STORY BEHIND BOOKS

## Where Do Books Come From?

It's undeniable that the majority of people interested in the publishing industry are, well, those who *work* in the publishing industry. But behind the production of books, yesterday and today, is a much larger story than the who-fired-whom struggles that get written about in the newspaper's book pages—who's getting an undeservedly large advance, which director of publicity is moving from one publisher to a rival, whether a massive marketing campaign is producing commensurate sales. (In short, who's up and who's down.)

Understanding where books come from, from the very beginning to today, puts them in perspective. You get a sense of how the books that you're interested in collecting—whether they're priceless gems or novelty items—fit into the overall picture. You learn what's been influential and what is forgotten, what was the biggest seller of its day, and what was banned in Boston.

Reading history highlights the fact, one easy to overlook, that nearly every one of the books that we treasure today was sent out into the world by a publisher that hoped the item would sell enough copies to turn a profit. "We do not always bear in mind," wrote W. Carew Hazlitt in *The Book-Collector* (1904), "that the rare books of to-day were the current literature [of] the period of their appearance."

The histories of both reading and publishing are truly fascinating; I hope this all-too-brief summary inspires you to follow up and read more in-depth.

### The Early History

By the time Johannes Gutenberg made history around 1450 by printing the first volumes using movable type, people already had been collecting books for two millennia. The ancient Greeks were consumed by "book madness," writes Nicholas Basbanes in *A Gentle Madness*, his history of bibliophilia. "Competition was keen, the hunt relentless, and the qualities so coveted now—good condition, scarcity, and significance—were equally prized twenty-five centuries ago."

Critics even made the same snarky jokes about accumulating books: that collectors were far more interested in quantity than quality, and in the volumes' value rather than their contents. The first-century Stoic poet Seneca complained that the great library of Alexandria was "not for study but for display." In a criticism that seems pointed and fresh today, he wrote, "Of what use are books without number and complete collections if their owner barely finds time in the course of his life even to read their titles?"

Of course, *book* meant something different to the ancients. The Greeks wrote on clay tablets until they began importing papyrus paper from Egypt around 600 B.C.E. As described in Lionel Casson's *Libraries in the Ancient World*, paper was used in rolls formed from twenty individual sheets of very roughly the same size as today's letter-size paper. Writing with a reed pen and lampblack ink, an author or scribe—a professional writer—might fill one scroll or, in the case of long works, many.

Initially, books were disseminated orally—few if any copies were made, and people would learn the contents only by attending readings. But a few decades later, a far more efficient—and lucrative—means of distribution was discovered: Copies of books could be made *and sold*. Soon booksellers were flourishing in Athens, with local customers competing with those from overseas.

With copies made by hand and therefore error-prone—and this being long before the invention of copyright, which preserves and protects texts' original state—some books were of higher quality than others, leading to a demand for the best copies available.

Greeks and Romans eventually moved from scrolls to wax tablets, which they began binding together with cords, producing the *codex*—the first reading matter to resemble, in basic form, today's books. Soon books were being written on parchment made from various materials, including leather, far less unwieldy than wax tablets.

Around 100 B.C.E. papermaking was invented in China and over the next millennium slowly made its way through the Middle East. Not until the thirteenth century did paper reach Italy. By the time Gutenberg introduced movable type—allowing multiple pages of a single book to be set using and reusing the same stock of type—to Europe, Chinese publishers had been using the technique for more than four centuries.

Some resisted the move to machine-printed books; Basbanes explains that "Florentine bibliophiles were fiercely proud of their calligraphic traditions, and did not warm immediately to the idea of books that were mass-produced." But as with today's technological innovations, lower cost and increased convenience carried the day, and the great tradition of hand-lettered volumes was relegated to museums.

With the introduction of dust jackets in the 1830s and the paperback in 1841 (by a German publisher), most of the elements of modern book publishing were in place.

## The Rise of the Publisher

The earliest books were published in the New World long before the United States came into being; the one considered the very first is the 1640 volume *The Whole Booke of Psalmes*, known as the "Bay Psalm Book," of which seventeen hundred copies were printed and only eleven survive.

Why are they so rare? Because not until the last two hundred years were most books considered objects to keep—they were often sold in unbound sheets, for the owner to have bound if he wanted to, or as cheap paperbacks. A century ago, Hazlitt lamented how few examples of early literature have survived: "Books, and more especially pamphlets and broadsheets, were acquired, and, after perusal, flung away," he wrote, explaining that the system of buying and selling was a recent invention. "There were not only no booksellers, in our sense, but down to the seventeenth century no systematic book-buyers."

The "Bay Psalm Book" was also typical in that the bulk of early books, around the world as well as in America, were religious in nature. Indeed, many American households owned no books apart from a Bible and a farmer's almanac. As literacy grew and interests expanded, so did demand for a wider range of books.

That's where publishers come in.

It seems a self-evident process: Getting a book from the author's pen, or typewriter, or PC, requires someone to actually print it, someone to sell it, and someone to broker the deal—in other words, to publish it. But it wasn't always so obvious: Important early figures such as Isaiah Thomas of Massachusetts played the roles of printer, publisher, *and* bookseller. Not until the nineteenth century were those roles sorted out and separated, and even today, there's plenty of crossover—consider Barnes & Noble's recent foray into publishing books that it then sells in stores, or university presses selling their own publications online.

In the 1810s, the first modern publishers—creating a unique catalog of books and "branding" them—arose in what remains the world capital of publishing: Manhattan. Indeed, the first two publishers, Harper's and John Wiley, are still thriving.

Some key American authors—Nathaniel Hawthorne, James Fenimore Cooper, and Edgar Allan Poe among them—flourished in the first part of the nineteenth century, but American book-buyers generally preferred English authors to those from their own shores. Publishers obliged, producing innumerable editions of popular overseas authors whether or not they had permission, owned the copyright, or intended to compensate the authors. American laws at the time were extremely lax, and citizens supported international copyright only in principle, since otherwise the price of books would rise.

Many of these classics and current books were produced in series with titles like Library of Choice Reading (Harper's) and Library of American Books (Wiley), which collected older classics as well. The 1870s saw other publishers get into the act, introducing the Lakeside Library, Seaside Library, Riverside Library, Home Library, and Fireside Library. In the twentieth century, publishers would create such enduring series as the Modern Library and Library of America.

Great novels and poetry—those we still read today—may have been popular, but just as is true today, they comprised a small fraction of the books sold. In addition to the usual Bibles and "cyclopedias," buyers snapped up popular science, history, pulpy "dime novels," general nonfiction, memoirs, and sentimental or "domestic" fiction that—not unlike today's romance novels—went down easily and left the reader craving more.

Despite selling literally millions of copies to American women, even the best-selling authors of sentimental novels, such as Mary Jane Holmes and E.D.E.N. Southworth, have been almost entirely forgotten.

In the middle of the flood of sentimental novels landed Harriet Beecher Stowe's brutal *Uncle Tom's Cabin*, which sold 305,000 copies in its first year and remains in print today, having sold in the neighborhood of 7 million copies.

Among all the publishers that arose to try their hand at bringing forth best-sellers throughout the nineteenth

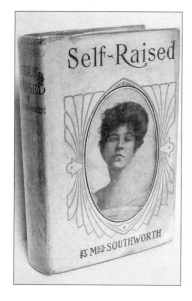

**"Domestic" Fiction** *(above left)*. Emma Dorothy Eliza Nevitte Southworth was one of the nineteenth century's best-selling authors.

**Still a Top Seller** *(above right)*. An 1852 first edition of *Uncle Tom's Cabin*.

century—and into the decades following—were many that survive today, albeit in different forms. Their founders, understandably, usually put their own names on the books' spines, and it's those names—among them Scribner, Dutton, Harcourt, Harper, Wiley, Putnam, Holt, Houghton, Knopf, Simon, and Schuster—that have passed into common usage.

## As We Know Them Today

In the nineteenth century, many books were sold not in stores but by subscription by door-to-door salesmen. Publishing historian John Tebbel notes that many of these books were "the tasteless products of hucksters"—printed on thick, cheap, oversize paper to seem more substantial than they were, with gaudy covers, and priced higher than necessary. We know today that bigger isn't necessarily better, but book-starved buyers a century ago had yet to learn the lesson.

From today's perspective, the subscription trend was a blessing: Any number of interesting titles appeared (and remain sporadically available today) that, because of their limited appeal or controversial content, no major publisher would have risked producing. And door-to-door sales unquestionably brought books to thousands of households that owned nothing more than the usual

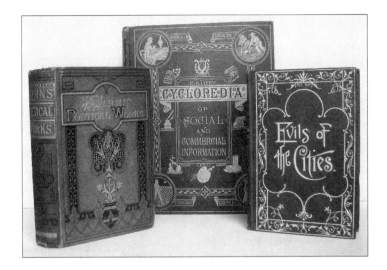

Bible and farmer's almanac. That's a positive step no matter how many crummy books were pawned off as valuable heirlooms-to-be.

Interest in reading was greatly aided by the rapid growth of public libraries, sponsored by industrialist Andrew Carnegie, who aimed to make books available to all Americans regardless of income.

And books themselves changed: In the 1870s, the publisher Dodd, Mead introduced color-ink stamping to book covers, and publishers began to compete for browsers' attention, with ever more elaborate designs as well as newly fervent marketing campaigns.

The efforts paid off in increased sales, particularly with regard to fiction—which, for the two decades following 1890, became "something of a mania," according to Tebbel.

After the chaos of World War I—during which, as bibliophile Holbrook Jackson notes, "books of all kinds were *pulped* by the ton to meet the paper shortage"—publishing picked itself up and hit its stride.

The period between the wars is often characterized as a "Golden Age of Publishing," a time when publishers emphasized personal vision over profits. This is undeniably an overly nostalgic view—profits have *always* been a pri-

**As We Know Them Today.** Before dust jackets, publishers used elaborate covers to draw book-buyers.

ority—but it's true that the era produced an unprecedented number of lasting authors and books. Several major publishers either began operating or hit their stride.

(Random House was founded in 1925; the name derives from founders Bennett Cerf and Donald Klopfer's desire to print fine, limited editions "at random." After the crash of 1929 and the end of the limited-editions craze, Random House moved into more conventional publishing.)

The era saw innovations in marketing and publishing and the introduction of paperback originals and pocketbooks. For the first time, sales of trade nonfiction overtook that of fiction—apparently for good.

## From Protection to Promotion

The 1920s also saw the establishment of dust jackets as a standard feature of hardcovers. Publishers had covered their books with paper jackets for decades—the earliest surviving DJ dates from 1832—but they weren't meant to be kept. As the name *dust jacket* implies, the covering was intended to protect the actual book until the buyer got it home . . . at which point he threw it away. This is why few jackets from the first two decades of the twentieth century survive and, when they do, they're typically plain and dull. There are plenty of exceptions—consider the famously eye-catching jackets adorning F. Scott Fitzgerald's novels—but most early DJs contain little in the way of either information or color.

But soon marketers began seeing the jackets as advertising space and adding information about other titles available from the publisher, along with testimonials. Then, in the 1920s, writes Michael Korda in *Making the List*, large bookstores changed the way they marketed and sold their wares, displaying books flat, on tables, rather than strictly on shelves, spines out. So publishers added artwork to their books' DJs, to help them stand out from competitors.

Even so, Tebbel notes, DJs were not universally popular. In 1926, literary critic William Lyon Phelps wrote, "I wish the publishers would quit putting jackets on their books. The first thing I do when I get a book is to throw the jacket away without reading it."

Book-buyers of the era often followed suit: Even though DJs became informative and were
often dazzling—with blurbs, descriptions, and author photos
and biographies—consumers
still tended to toss them out.
This is doubly a shame: Comparatively few books from those
decades still have their DJs, and
the books themselves typically
sport dull boards.

## The Postwar Period

After World War II, a series of
mergers, acquisitions, and consolidations changed the
industry's emphasis, putting the great houses under the
umbrella of various conglomerates with no previous
connection to publishing.

**From
Protection to
Promotion.**
Typical DJs
from the days
before
marketers had
discovered their
potential.

Since the industry's beginnings, publishers had bought,
sold, and merged with their rivals and colleagues—indeed, mergers produced many of the great imprints. But
this was different: For the first time, the people control-
ling the production of books were not "book people"—
that is, inveterate readers who stayed in the profession
out of the desire to contribute to the world of letters. In
*The Book in America*, Richard W. Clement laments "the
takeover of virtually all the major houses by larger corpo-
rations, organizations with no understanding or respect
for the traditions of publishing and whose major motiva-
tion was profit."

From readers' perspective, not much changed: New
books continued to appear, with a familiar-seeming mix
of new and established authors; bookstore shelves didn't
go empty.

But inside the industry, everything was different: Many of
the publishers founded by men with dreams of literary
immortality became assembly lines pushing product at
consumers. Companies with distinct visions came
under broad corporate umbrellas and became amor-
phous. Editors and designers and marketing managers
began moving freely between the publishers, since they

no longer had distinct identities. It became difficult to re-call which multinational corporation owned which publisher.

Incidentally, House of Collectibles (the publisher listed on the spine of this book) is an imprint of Random House Information Group, itself a division of Random House, the world's largest publishing empire. And even Random House has a corporate parent: It was bought by RCA in 1965, which sold it to Advance Publications in 1980, which sold it to Bertelsmann in 1998.

In the eyes of detractors, many publishers have been buried under layers of corporate management—and at the top, too many people who tend to see books as just another commodity. "It is now increasingly the case that the owner's *only* interest is in making money and as much of it as possible," writes André Schiffrin, a long-time publisher and critic who bemoans the shift from "worthwhile books" to "books based on lifestyle and celebrity with little intellectual or artistic merit."

Publishers continue to bring out more topnotch titles than the public can read, and most of the editors who sift through book proposals and sweat over manuscripts love their jobs. The corporate influence has left the spirit of those who work with words largely intact. But it's small wonder that observers fondly recall the industry's simpler, pre-takeover days.

## Who Publishes Books?
Book publishing, writes Jason Epstein in *Book Business: Publishing Past, Present, and Future*, "is not a conventional business. It more closely resembles a vocation or an amateur sport in which the primary goal is the activity itself rather than its financial outcome."

For most collectors—as well as for people who read books and have some general interest in the publishing industry—the bulk of the attention goes to fiction and, to a lesser extent, high-profile nonfiction. People "believe that publishing is trade books, bookstores, best-seller lists, and reviews," notes historian John Tebbel.

But that's only part of the story: English-language publishers bring out some 150,000 new titles every year, and the majority of those—not to mention the bulk of publishers' profits—belong not to literary fiction but to much less sexy sectors, such as textbooks and reference books, and to the business- and religion-books shelves. People generally see only "the tip of the publishing iceberg," Tebbel writes. The whole picture shows a scene far more sprawling and balkanized: "By far the largest part of the book publishing business is embodied in that great complex of companies and activities producing educational, business, scientific, technical, and reference books and materials."

How many books are in circulation right now, out there in the world? Billions, certainly, in this country alone. It's impossible to say with any certainty, since the number changes constantly. David S. and Susan Siegel of Book Hunter Press estimate that North American used-book dealers currently offer more than 100 million books.

Those numbers are reason to rejoice—*all those books!*—or, perhaps, pine for simpler days. Writing a century ago, W. Carew Hazlitt lamented the explosion of available books: "Happy the men who lived before literary societies, book-clubs, and cheap editions, which have between them so multiplied the aggregate stock or material from which the collector has to make his choice!" Imagine what Hazlitt's attitude would have been toward eBay.

## Meet the Publishers

*Trade publishers* produce most of the books you see: hardcovers, trade paperbacks, pocketbooks. They may bring out specialized titles as well, but their emphasis is "the trade"—that is, general book-buyers.

Publishers call their big-budget would-be best-sellers *lead* titles; the books they assume will sell fewer copies are dubbed *midlist* titles. An author consigned to midlist status is pretty much on her own in terms of marketing and promotion, and most of these books will vanish with barely a trace. (For collectors, though, the best finds are great midlist titles, since they're far less common than lead books, and you can, in a sense, *discover* them.)

Hardcover fiction draws the most press, well out of proportion to its sales. A handful of blockbusters—most by established, heavily promoted authors—sell a ton each year and leave the mistaken impression that literary book sales are thriving. Interestingly, in both fiction and non-fiction, many "best-sellers" are far more widely discussed than read or purchased. Most titles don't sell out their first printings, and plenty of titles by celebrated authors sell startlingly few copies.

*Specialty publishers* produce books that the general press rarely writes about: textbooks, guidebooks, reference titles, novelty items, graphic novels, professional books for specific industries or professions. They may sell ten copies or tens of thousands, but anyone who doesn't seek them out may remain unaware of their existence.

You'll never see most religious publishers' titles unless you walk into a religious bookstore, or auto-repair manuals or technical business books unless you venture into unfamiliar bookshop aisles, or most children's books until you make your way to the corner of Borders with the life-size Barney and the storytelling clown.

*University presses* are publishers run by, well, universities. The first university press was established at Cornell in 1869, and many were established in the 1910s, primarily to provide a way for professors to publish their research. Then as now, at most colleges, professors seeking tenure must produce a book by their seventh or so year of teaching.

The publishers' primary function is to produce books for academic use—college libraries, scholars, classroom instruction. Many university presses publish dozens of books every year intended for small readerships, with little hope of best-sellerdom. Sometimes, depending on the author and topic, only a few hundred copies are printed (and perhaps more in softcover). Some presses— Oxford, Chicago, Princeton, Cambridge, California, Yale, Minnesota, Harvard, and a handful of others—also publish titles intended for wider readership, and a few of those *do* become best-sellers. And once in a great while, one of these books becomes truly collectible.

*Small presses* aim at niche audiences—often targeting readers through direct mail—and don't expect to sell

books by the boatload. They may concentrate on Chicano memoirs, or neo-segregationist screeds, or inspirational poetry, or lesbian-themed short stories, or African-American personal-finance guidebooks, or essays on the illegitimacy of the Bush administration. Over the last half-century, as trade publishers have become ever more indistinguishable and corporate, small presses have taken on a larger role in publishing.

*Vanity or "subsidy" presses* exist for aspiring authors who can't convince a publisher to bring out their books or, for whatever reason, prefer to handle the whole process themselves. Indeed, authors have self-published throughout the history of books, for one of three reasons: They feel they have something important to say, and no publisher will take a chance on their book; they're wealthy and tickled by the idea of being able to hand colleagues a book with their name on it; or they believe they can better control and market their book on their own.

Sometimes the author goes to the trouble of taking on a publisher's role and dealing with the laborious tasks of a book's production and distribution; other times, he or she will simply hook up with a vanity or "subsidy" press. With these, the author pays a company to edit, produce, market, and distribute a book. Since newspapers and magazines rarely review vanity-press books, few sell well

**University Presses.** Modern books published under the auspices of universities.

enough to earn back the money that the author pays the publisher, but that's to be expected. (For an inside look at the world of vanity publishing, I highly recommend Martin Amis's hilarious novel *The Information*.)

Are vanity-press books ever worth buying? Only very occasionally. A handful of these books are somewhat collectible—and many look interesting, sporting provocative and even inflammatory titles—but the majority are books that, well, only the author could love. And here's a warning: The name of the best-known vanity publisher, Vantage Press, is uncomfortably similar to both Vintage and Vanguard, two legitimate publishing imprints. As for the new breed of vanity-press books— those produced on demand through Xlibris, iUniverse, and the like: It's hard to envision these being collectible in any sense, since supply and demand are perfectly matched—when there's fresh demand for a single copy, the publisher prints one.

## Joining the Club

Since the advent of bookselling, millions of people have gotten their reading fix not from the local bookstore clerk but from the postman. For decades, door-to-door salesmen offered books in installments and via subscriptions, a personal but unreliable system. Enter the book club, which eased the passage from publisher to reader, particularly in regions of the country without ready access to stores.

The publishing industry embraced book clubs in the first years of the twentieth century, and the most successful and lasting clubs, the Literary Guild and Book-of-the-Month Club, were founded in the 1920s and continue to thrive.

Also in that decade came the rise of reprints, driven by the Doubleday publishing house, which bought the Literary Guild, created the Book League of America and other clubs, and founded the Triangle and Sun Dial reprint lines. By reaching consumers at all price levels, from high-quality new releases to inexpensive reprints, Doubleday squeezed every last sale from each title. Some of these were sold in drugstores and other nonstandard venues, but many made their way to readers in the post.

For any number of ambitious middle-class American families, Book-of-the-Month Club and other middle- and highbrow series of books (think of the Harvard Classics' "Five-Foot Shelf" and Britannica's "Great Books and Great Ideas" series) guaranteed that their homes would be regularly stocked with quality literature. With a prestigious committee giving its stamp of approval to only select books, BOMC helped shape the course of reading in America for decades.

BOMC's literary standards remain high—though the intellectual cachet of membership has faded—and the model of convenience remains attractive. Fifteen years ago, Tebbel estimated that more than 7 million Americans subscribed to book clubs, and since then plenty of new ones have arisen to take advantage of fresh pockets of interest: Consider the success of such clubs as Black Expressions (African-American), the Conservative Book Club, Crossings (Christian), the Doubleday Erotic Book Club, the History Book Club, the Military Book Club, and One Spirit (spirituality).

Others—most prominently the Stage & Screen Book Club, which began in 1950 as The Fireside Theatre—have called it quits in recent years, as those readers have become accustomed to acquiring books through other methods. But clearly the demise of the club concept is many years in the future.

## When New Books Don't Sell
Unique among American businesses, the publishing industry is saddled with a bizarre sales practice adopted during the Great Depression, when publishers convinced booksellers to carry their books by agreeing to take on much of the risk for their books not selling. The policy, still in effect today, means that sellers, often after just ninety days, can return unsold books to the publisher, making the retail bookselling business akin to consignment.

Considering the 150,000 new titles published each year, sellers have little incentive to keep books on shelves longer than necessary; they ship 'em right back to their place of origin.

What happens to all those books—and to the millions of others sitting in publishers' warehouses that never make

it to stores at all? Most of them become *remainders*. These are some of the books you see on bargain-books shelves at the chain stores, or in the Daedalus or Edward R. Hamilton mail-order catalogs. Their status is usually indicated by a dot or stripe at the top or bottom of a book's text block.

There's no shame in a book's being remaindered—after all, nearly every single trade book gets remaindered at some point

**When New Books Don't Sell.** Remaindered books, to be offered at a discount.

in its life. A hit novel can go through twenty printings and sell out all of them, but if sales peter out on the twenty-first, someone gets stuck with the extras—and they'll surely turn up in a $3.99 bin.

Naturally, the most common remainders are the books that *really* didn't sell, those for which the publisher vastly overestimated demand. A book's commercial failure often has little to do with its quality—circumstances and timing may conspire against it. Perhaps it's a story of a headline-grabbing crime that turns out to be prema-ture—there's a major break in the case just before publi-cation—and the book limps into stores. Or maybe a competing publisher brings out a rival book on the same topic, winning the race to publication and exhausting in-terest. Or a sinking economy or distracting news event means that everyone stops buying *any* books for a few months.

Or, for instance, after an author has a hit, she is usually able to negotiate a larger first printing for the follow-up. But book-buyers are fickle, and follow-ups seldom make as big a splash. The result, more often than not, is stacks of hardcovers of the sequel winding up on bargain shelves.

Since readers and collectors often discover books long after they've hit remainder bins, many desirable titles are often found with dots or stripes. They're worth maybe 10 or 20 percent less than unmarked copies, depending in part on the mark's unsightliness.

## Collecting Through the Ages

The modern history of collecting is largely that of rich men building massive collections, spending millions at auction to capture items of nearly unimaginable rarity and significance: association copies inscribed by John Milton, first printings of Shakespeare, handwritten volumes of Dante. When you read, say, Basbanes's *A Gentle Madness*, you may get the nagging feeling that one can't be a real collector without infinite free time, two country homes just for storage, and the kind of wealth possessed only by dot-com CEOs who cashed out before the crash.

And indeed, after reading about legendary books and 100,000-title collections, it's somewhat harder to get excited about discovering a library-sale first edition of *The Lovely Bones*. So try to think of that level of collecting as something entirely distinct from what you're doing— after all, if you begin to compare your situation to those of the "great" collectors, you'll be too intimidated to collect *anything*.

In short: Both you and library patron Samuel P. Huntington have been interested in collecting books—but you're not really participating in the same hobby.

### From the Beginning

The first great book collector was the fourth-century B.C.E. Greek philosopher Aristotle, who compiled a personal library so much vaster than his contemporaries' that he needed to invent a system of organization. Several decades later, the leaders of Greek-controlled Egypt planned a great public repository of books in the new city of Alexandria and began purchasing—and pilfering— other collections to build a giant library that held every known book in existence.

In those 2,500 years since, dozens of bibliophiles and bibliomaniacs have striven to compile private libraries of lasting significance. Some have aimed for high volume; perhaps most notable is Richard Heber, who in the early nineteenth century attended every auction he could and ended up with something over 150,000 books, a library filling *eight houses* in five countries. It's still considered the largest private collection ever assembled.

More common has been those who have, by virtue of massive wealth, been able to compile "high-spot" collections that include copies of the most desirable items: Poe, Shakespeare, Milton, etc. In flush times, more people have been able to enter the hobby in a major way, which is when Gutenberg Bibles change hands. For instance, the years 1870 to 1929 were a "Golden Age" of collecting in the United States, in which "the building of great libraries became an emblem of wisdom and accomplishment," Basbanes writes.

Unsurprisingly, the 1929 crash and the Great Depression wiped out book values and collectors' enthusiasm along with their stock portfolios, and the high prices of the late 1920s didn't recover for a decade.

### Evaluating Values

Over the decades, prices for first editions of great, established authors have slowly, steadily risen—and yet this is not a hobby for investors, particularly short-termers. Money can be made buying and selling books, but the risks shouldn't be underestimated. "It is true that good books bought wisely have proven to be solid investments over the years," writes Nicholas Basbanes in *Among the Gently Mad*, "but there is a wild card in the mix, and that is the fickle nature of fashion."

Indeed, literary historians chronicle how authors have been in and out of style—sometimes inexplicably—and their value to collectors follows suit. In the 1920s, notes John Carter in *Taste & Technique in Book Collecting*, collectors drove up prices of James M. Barrie and John Galsworthy books while ignoring those of Virginia Woolf and E.M. Forster. In the decades following, they changed their minds: Today Barrie and Galsworthy are widely ignored; Woolf and Forster are top collectibles.

Carter notes that patterns in collecting have often followed those in reading—"the periodic fluctuation of literary (and to some extent of social) taste." Writing in 1947, he traces recent history: "The Romantics revolted from the Age of Reason, the Victorians from the Regency, the Nineties from the Victorians; the Elizabethan and Jacobean dramatists were rediscovered at the beginning of the nineteenth century, the Romantics at its end, the Victorians in our own time; and we may confidently expect that the pattern will repeat itself . . . so long as literature is read and studied."

Other reasons why a particular author's or book's value may rise:

- Sometimes a movie adaptation has a major impact, as with Winston Groom's *Forrest Gump*, other times almost none. Occasionally, even a film that almost no one sees sparks interest: The 2001 movie *Iris* directed renewed attention to the novels of Iris Murdoch.

- Latter-day authors and critics sometimes champion an out-of-print author or particular book, in an effort to restore a reputation. Recent examples: Dawn Powell (promoted by Gore Vidal), Jincy Willett (David Sedaris), Richard Yates (Richard Ford and Richard Russo), and Glenway Wescott (Michael Cunningham, Susan Sontag, and Jeffrey Eugenides).

- A new biography, such as Larry Lockridge's 1994 *Shade of the Raintree*, about his father, *Raintree County* author Ross Lockridge Jr. Even a magazine article can do it, as when a compelling 1994 *New Yorker* profile of novelist James Wilcox brought him unexpected attention. Though each of Wilcox's novels had sold only a few thousand copies in hardcover, the new interest generated trade-paperback printings of many times that number (though, interestingly, not higher values for those uncommon first editions).

- A hit book may spike the author's earlier and scarcer titles: As just one example, Cormac McCarthy's 1992 bestseller *All the Pretty Horses* drove his first novel, 1965's *The Orchard Keeper*, from $75 to $2,000 practically overnight, and prices for even his 1980s novels rose to well over $1,000 each.

**Evaluating Values.** Those who invested in first editions by John Galsworthy and James M. Barrie back in the 1920s were kicking themselves by the 1940s.

- And sometimes, as with stock prices, there's no apparent reason why a book's value begins to rise—just that all of a sudden collectors and dealers note an increased demand and climbing prices.

Just as values can rise, though, they can slowly fall. Perusing old price guides, such as William Targ's 1941 *American Books and Their Prices*, is guaranteed to produce wistfulness: A first of William Faulkner's *Light in August* went for $3.50! You could buy a first of *The Adventures of Huckleberry Finn* for $75! And yet the vast majority of titles and authors that Targ listed—books that dealers were selling regularly to collectors—are completely unfamiliar today to anyone save the serious professional. That's not to say that the books aren't still collectible in a general sense, but they sure weren't drop-dead great investments.

Sometimes, the nature of the market itself creates ups and downs. Seattle bookseller Phil Arundel compares collectors to investors who buy stock either to hold (holders) or to sell for a quick profit (traders). "Ten years ago," he says, "there were literally hundreds of doctors, lawyers, and business executives running around buying up multiple copies of books with original lithographs by major artists such as Chagall and Miro. They would walk through our door and ask the same basic question, and they would discuss the current market price like it was IBM common stock. What typically happens in cases like this is that the real collectors—holders—are priced out of the market as prices rise. Rising prices draw more traders, who know that prices are foolishly high but believe that, when they want to sell, there will still be a 'greater fool' around as a buyer.

"Typically, all the traders try to sell at the same time, and prices drop like a rock," Arundel continues. "Eventually they fall to the point where real collectors can afford to buy again." The key, then, as with stock trading, is to do your homework, pay attention to trends in purchasing and values, and buy when prices are low.

### Collectors in a New Century
Today's collectors run the gamut, as they always have, from auction-going millionaires to flea-market browsers.

The Internet has vastly enlarged the pool of available books and widened the range of prices, allowing collectors at the lower-priced end to participate in the hobby more fully than ever before.

Women, too, are now fully fledged partners, participants, and competitors, as anyone who frequents bookstores and book sales will attest. This is quite a shift: Though several women have had a lasting impact on the hobby—for instance, Amy Lowell, who donated her astonishing Keats collection to Harvard in 1925—the vast majority of serious book collectors have, historically, been men, which is no surprise, considering the financial resources required.

The well-documented achievements of a handful of prominent African-American bibliophiles will likely inspire collectors of other backgrounds and ethnicities to explore fields that have not traditionally seen as collectible.

Plenty of rich collectors continue to participate, of course. The booms of the 1980s and 1990s created new wealth and new buyers for art, antiques, and, naturally, books. Some holders of literary treasures took advantage of the high-flying market and offered long-unseen items at auction, which meant that highly prized gems changed hands, passing from one magnificent library to another.

But the most inspiring stories have been, and continue to be, of those collectors who, through passion and effort, have built specialized libraries that became the finest of their kind—collections that are more than the sum of their parts.

Collectors don't, of course, *create* books—what they do is compile, redistribute, and disseminate them. Building a collection is itself an act of creation, and the situation today—more books on more subjects with lower prices—provides unprecedented opportunity to create something truly special.

"It's a great time to collect, because of the Internet," says Ken Eastman of Moe's Books in Berkeley. "Because almost everything is now common, prices have plummeted. And it's a great time if you have obscure interests or are amassing a library. Before the Internet, trying to find a particular rare book could have been a lifelong hunt; you might never have found it. Now you just type it into a database, and there it is.

"It's a golden age for buyers."

## Where Do the Great Collections Go?

Fortunately for book-hunters, as yet no significant bibliophile has demanded that his library follow him to the grave. Some have donated intact collections to libraries or museums, fearing what one called the "disaster of dispersion." Others have asked that their collections be sold at auction after their death, so that the books may return to circulation and enrich others' personal libraries. "If the great collections of the past had not been sold," asked collector Robert Hoe III, who died in 1909 and left instructions for his library's dispersal, "where would I have found my books?"

Thirteenth-century bibliophile Richard de Bury stipulated that his collection go to Oxford University; the Rev. John Harvard's 329 titles, donated to an as-yet-unnamed college being built near Boston, began the first library in North America; for $23,950, Thomas Jefferson sold his 6,487 books to the United States itself, for the purposes of rebuilding the British-destroyed Library of Congress; many of the rare-book rooms that adorn American college libraries are filled with donated treasures.

Your collection may not be so grand as all that—few personal libraries are genuinely museum-worthy. But it's worth thinking about: Where would you like your collection to end up? Remember that your books will outlive you—you're merely holding onto them for a while, adding value by protecting them and making them a part of your collection.

Not that you need to keep in the forefront of your mind how your heirs will dispose of your library after your death! Really, it's enough that you enjoy your books now.

## The Author's Touch: Autographs, Authenticity, and Association Copies

Why do we find authors' autographs desirable? If a first edition signifies the first appearance of a new set of

In "The ...s of an ...tuff, who ...tion in a ...p," he ...tor and ...Presley ...cribes ...r- ...ust- ...y. he ...tween

**Greasy Lake**
& Other Stories

T. Coraghessan Boyle

Viking

ideas, an autograph signifies one step closer to the ideas' genesis: The author actually *held* this particular book, and the autograph is the proof.

**The Author's Touch.** T.C. Boyle's bold stroke.

On his website, novelist T.C. Boyle wryly ruminates on why fans and collectors come to author signings: "[T]he experience of the signing—the recollection of the moment, of the reading that preceded it, of the era in one's own life during which the reading/signing took place— make it a very satisfactory thing all the way around. And plus, you do have a flake of the writer too, this physical sputtering weak little line of a signature limping across the page." (I should note that Boyle's signature is neither "sputtering," "weak," nor "little.")

Signing events can be fun, but even an autograph that you don't get in person carries value both monetary and sentimental. It can make a common book far less common, even unique.

How much is a signature worth? The range is vast. Books on collecting often offer guidelines on how much value an author's autograph adds to a book—$5, $10, 10 percent, 20 percent, whatever—but this advice is not re-

Don't Tell Dad

HYPERION

Peter [signature] '98

**Inscribed vs. Plain Signature.** Peter Fonda autographed this bookplate but likely never laid eyes on the book itself.

motely helpful. There is no rule whatsoever: With any given book or author, an autograph's value may add hundreds of dollars in value or nothing at all. A sociologist's book about Arkansas office workers is likely worth the same signed or plain; Katharine Hepburn's autobiography is worth just a few dollars unadorned but several hundred signed.

## Inscribed vs. Plain Signature

There's a question—it doesn't quite rise to the level of a debate—about whether a book is more desirable with a simple autograph or with an author inscription to some unknown previous owner. For me, the more writing from an author's pen, the better. "As far as I am concerned, a message of some sort is the far more interesting choice," agrees Nicholas Basbanes, "for the simple fact that there is more *writing*."

If an autograph signifies a direct, hands-on connection between book and author, an inscription—no matter to whom—means an even closer connection, more contact with the book, more of a *moment*. It means that the author (certainly not an assistant or secretary) signed the book not as an anonymous one pulled off the top of a stack but as a particular copy, handed to a particular person.

Any kind of autograph on any page is considered far preferable to a signature on a bookplate or one that's *tipped in*, since either means that the author didn't actually hold this particular copy.

Among other terms you may run across: *Hand signed* and *signed in person* mean only that it wasn't done by an autopen or secretary, which are possibilities with just a handful of authors (e.g., U.S. presidents or superstar athletes). *Flatsigned*, a term that originated in the sports-autographs world and whose use in bookselling has grown over the last decade, is a synonym—an unnecessary one—for *plain autograph*.

As for an author writing the date alongside the signature: This is desirable, far more so when the date is close to the book's publication. A book signed in the year of publication is good, in the month of publication is better, and best of all is one signed on the very day of—or, in the case of an advance reading copy, *before*—publication.

## Associating with the Author

An *association copy* is a book owned by someone important to the author and evidenced by a bookplate or inscription. If an autograph is a tiny piece of the author, an association inscription is a glimpse into the author's life, a piece of a relationship. It is, by definition, unique.

In terms of desirability, the closer ties the author and addressee have, the better; the greater stature both have, the better; the more relevant the book is to the relationship, the better. At the least, the author must have some actual connection to the addressee: If I inscribe a copy of *Instant Expert: Collecting Books* to Madonna or Bill Gates, that doesn't automatically imbue it with inestimable value.

It's always a little embarrassing to both signer and recipient when the latter has clearly just discarded the book, when the relationship is nakedly unrequited. Easily the most notorious case arose in 1996, when novelist Paul

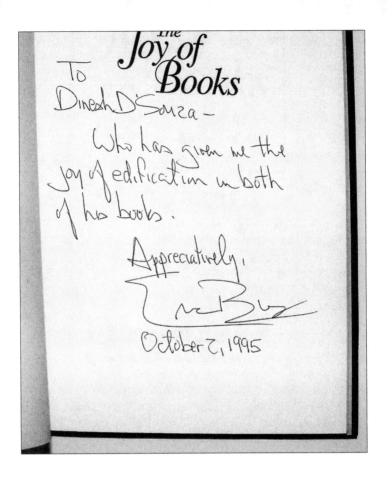

The Joy of Books

To
Dinesh D'Souza —
Who has given me the
joy of edification in both
of his books.

Appreciatively,

October 2, 1995

**Associating with the Author.** Dinesh D'Souza didn't keep his presentation copy of Eric Burns' *The Joy of Books* for long.

Theroux came across a rare-book catalog listing of a book he had inscribed to his longtime mentor, V.S. Naipaul, who had evidently decided to sell all his autographed Theroux books—publicly. The listing signaled the end of the friendship and inspired Theroux's blistering memoir *Sir Vidia's Shadow*.

The most personal and unique copy of all is what some call the *dedication copy*: inscribed by the author to the book's dedicatee. But it's fun to speculate on the most desirable imaginable association copies: Ernest Hemingway inscribing *To Have and Have Not* to Humphrey Bogart? Helen Keller's *The Story of My Life* to Theodore Roosevelt? John Lennon's *In His Own Write* to Paul McCartney? William Shakespeare's *Hamlet* to King James?

## Getting Your Books Signed

Apart from buying books already signed, how do you get autographs in the first place? After all, not every American lives in Manhattan or Los Angeles, where most touring authors stop. And most authors don't tour widely, or at all.

Well, you can still use the bookshops that the authors *do* visit. Many stores that regularly hold signings (such as Cody's in Berkeley, Book Soup in West Hollywood, Tattered Cover in Denver, and A Clean Well-Lighted Place for Books in San Francisco) will gladly take pre-orders for autographed first editions and ship copies.

It's a more rewarding experience, of course, to actually attend signings. Not only will you have the memory of a reading and meeting the author—you can get signatures on your copies of the author's previous books and, time permitting, even personal inscriptions.

How many books can you legitimately set in front of an author and expect autographs? "Generally speaking," admonishes Robert A. Wilson, "two or at the most three books is as many as one should ask to have signed at a time." This is a good rule at some heavily managed events that draw hundreds of fans and autograph lines around the block. At those, the author or bookstore may limit signed books to one or two per person.

But at most readings, there's far more flexibility, much as the cramped-wristed author might wish otherwise. At moderately attended signings, three is a reasonable maximum if you're hoping for personal inscriptions, five if you prefer just a signature. And in my experience, few authors mind signing stacks of books for bright-eyed fans—as opposed to impatient dealers—who considerately wait at the end of the line.

If you have contact information for an author, you can certainly send a letter or e-mail and inquire into the possibilities of mailing books to have signed. You may have better luck going through the author's agent or publicist; try phoning the publisher, asking for the publicity department, and tracking down the right person. Never just mail books without getting an OK beforehand, and make sure you've made the process of returning the signed books to you as easy as possible: sufficient postage, self-addressed packaging, etc.

## Supply and Oversupply

Values are, once again, all about supply and demand. A popular author who makes annual, big-city public appearances and cheerfully signs any item handed to her will make many loyal fans—but will certainly lower the value of her autograph, since anyone who wants one can have one.

Hence the low prices assigned to signed books by crime-thriller authors such as Carl Hiaasen, James Lee Burke, and Lisa Scottoline; novelists Robert Olen Butler and Richard Paul Evans; humorist Dave Barry; and entertainment personalities Lawrence Welk, Helen Hayes, and Sophie Tucker. (Pulitzer-winning novelist Michael Chabon is wonderfully friendly and seems to enjoy the author-tour process so much that he's on the verge of flooding the collectibles market with signed books.)

The bargain prices are no indication of sinking popularity with readers—only with collectors. After all, when anyone who wants a signed copy of *Dave Barry in Cyberspace* can have one for five bucks, the book doesn't have much appeal left.

There are plenty of inconsistencies: Some books by particular authors are far more common signed than others. You can tell by how often particular books show up on eBay—and find no buyers at any price—that the authors toured widely. Hence the seeming omnipresence of autographed copies of Don Winslow's *The Death and Life of Bobby Z* and Jane Smiley's *The All-True Travels and Adventures of Lidie Newton*

Occasionally, it doesn't require an in-person tour to spike supply through the roof. Knopf gave crime-thriller star James Ellroy's riveting 1996 memoir, *My Dark Places*, a fifty-thousand-copy first printing, and the author autographed every one of those copies. The result is that there are far fewer *unsigned* copies of the book than *signed*, and that Ellroy's autograph no longer carries the cachet it did. Likewise, rock star Gene Simmons autographed the first forty thousand copies of his 2003 book *Sex Money Kiss*, promptly devaluing his signature—

though, since his band Kiss has a few more than forty thousand fans, even that many autographs won't completely satisfy the demand.

Some authors who rise to an extreme level of popularity understandably begin limiting their appearances—since they don't need to tour to generate interest and sales—and, therefore, the availability of signed books. John Irving decided some years ago to no longer sign books in the United States. (He explains why in his novel *A Widow for One Year*, through his protagonist.) Though Irving's autograph is hardly scarce, that decision itself raised its value.

## Who Wants 'Em?

So much for supply. Now, why the demand for some autographs and not others?

We're back to intangibles. No collector has decreed which authors' signatures are valuable—it all has to do with how interested buyers are in those signatures. And there's no rule or, often, even a rationale why one obscure but well-thought-of writer is highly sought-after and a comparable contemporary is not. But that's one more reason why this is such a fascinating and complex hobby.

By far the biggest fluctuations in price are for books signed by celebrities of any stripe. Predictably, their value peaks within weeks of the book's release and then slowly wanes. To take just a few examples in one subject area, let's look at what's happened to autographed memoirs of a few prominent political figures.

In 1995, Newt Gingrich, speaker of the House of Representatives, toured for his book *To Renew America*, hastily compiled at the apex of his meteoric rise in popularity, and newspapers documented the hundreds of fans queuing at each tour stop, clutching armloads of $24 hardcovers to get a scrawled "Newt" on each one. Three years later, Gingrich resigned amid scandal and disgrace, and today those signed books go for $5 each. As for the countless copies of *To Renew America* that *aren't* signed: The going rate on Amazon is just a penny—still overvalued, if you ask me.

Several years later, we learned more than we wanted to know about Clinton intern Monica Lewinsky, and peo-

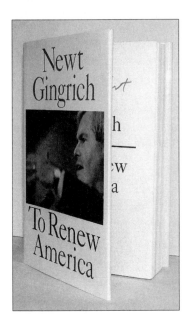

**Who Wants 'Em?** A signed Newt Gingrich book—at $5, still not a bargain.

ple gathered in droves to get their own signed copies of *Monica* (with full-name autographs worth more, naturally, than just "Monica"). On eBay, those copies soared. Today, the craze seems absurd: Just who were the people who paid $200 each for books autographed by Monica Lewinsky? Surely they *knew*, deep down, that two years hence *Monica* would be worth only about the book's cover price—and I wouldn't count on it holding even *that* value.

Mired in an ugly divorce and plummeting popularity, New York City mayor Rudy Giuliani rose to the occasion when the attacks of September 11, 2001, stunned the nation, and that nation took note. Giuliani rushed out a book titled *Leadership* and held New York signing events, and eBay prices hit the stratosphere . . . only to fall back to earth when the shock wore off.

A month after the 2003 publication of her memoir *Living History*, U.S. Senator Hillary Clinton estimated that she had autographed some twenty thousand books, so many that her hand had gone numb at several signing events. That's not quite 2 percent of the copies sold by that point, but it'll likely be enough to satisfy demand down the road, driving down the book's value—unless, of course, Clinton runs for president in 2008 or 2012, at which point all bets are off.

A few more thoughts about the value of autographed books:

• The one category of autographed political books that *are* consistently valuable is those by U.S. presidents, with the exceptions of Herbert Hoover, who remained a statesman and public figure for decades after his unpopular term in office, and Jimmy Carter, who has authored more than a dozen books.

- Unless they're written by celebrity authors, nonfiction books often carry no extra value when autographed. The same goes for books by clergymen or academics.

- Considering their authors' influence and pervasiveness, autographed books by news personalities such as Dan Rather, Hugh Downs, and David Frost are worth surprisingly little.

- As with sports cards, signed books by sports stars seem to have value based on the author's personal popularity rather than statistics or credentials. Autographs by a few players—most prominently Yankees star Mickey Mantle—carry a real premium; plenty of Hall of Famers (such as K.C. Jones and Sparky Anderson) are worth little if anything. The still-expanding sports-collectibles market has both ballooned the supply of autographs and, in essence, fixed the value of any given signature, but since the fans who buy signed 8x10s and baseballs don't seem to have much interest in books, the markets have little overlap.

## The Authenticity Issue

How do you know a signature is genuine? You can't be 100 percent certain unless you actually hand a book to the author and watch her scribble her name on the title page. In just about any other case, a really determined scam artist can fake whatever modern-era autograph is necessary. Even if a seller includes a snapshot of the author purportedly autographing *this very book*, you don't know for sure—he could be signing a different book, or it might have been taken by someone else, or taken at another time altogether.

What this means is that there is inherently a level of trust involved in buying autographed books, and you have to use common sense and a gut feeling. If you're looking at a fairly obscure item purportedly signed by a generally unknown author and offered on eBay for five bucks, chances are it's legit—why should the seller lie?

By contrast, a new signed copy of a celebrity memoir—particularly one going for mega-bucks—deserves close scrutiny. Seattle bookseller Phil Arundel warns that inflated values of autographed books—"the selling price is often many multiples of what an unsigned copy would bring"—may lead unscrupulous sellers to add a Sharpie scribble and offer a book as an "as-is" autographed copy. "Buyers are often guided by a personal passion and truly *want* to believe," he says, "and are just as happy with what they have as with a real example—until they try to sell the book years later."

Easily the most common phony signature is that of Stephen King, who signs a great many books but makes few in-store appearances, so his autograph is largely unavailable to those without access to his expensive limited editions.

But in my experience, amateur sellers present a bigger problem than forgery concerns: They sometimes present a book bearing an illegible scribble as authentically autographed. When you send a stern e-mail noting that the smudge on the half-title page in no way resembles the author's signature, the book's seller is often apologetic and even chagrined—and immediately offers a refund.

Sometimes you get a surreal argument: A recent eBay seller tried to pawn off a signed copy of *Seinlanguage* as "autographed by Jerry Seinfeld himself." When I pointed out that her book was merely previously owned by some guy named Lenny, she was indignant: "What makes you think this is not Jerry's autograph? I do believe it is. He is left-handed and that is the way he signs [his] name." I located a few credible Seinfeld signatures on the Web and e-mailed them, and the seller sheepishly refunded my money. "I really thought that was Jerry's autograph," she wrote.

An "Autographed Book" sticker on the dust jacket, while hardly definitive—you can buy the things, after all—is one tipoff that an autograph is likely genuine, particularly if it's from a particular store: Barnes & Noble, Borders, and Duck Soup have recognizable stickers.

Buying from an experienced and reputable dealer, one who guarantees his books, provides a measure of security. There's still a bit of faith involved—how does *he* know for sure?—but you should feel pretty confident. Unfortunately, buyers pay extra for that assurance: You won't catch an experienced antiquarian dealer drastically underpricing a signed collectible.

With amateurs or general bookstore owners, you can always ask about the provenance of an autograph, but for the vast majority of books, provenance may be murky or simply unavailable; particularly with older books, the seller probably isn't the original owner.

How can you at least *try* to find out whether a signature is real? If you need to know immediately—say, in deciding whether to bid in an eBay auction—start by searching online-store sites such as Advanced Book Exchange for signed books by the author, and hope that at least one includes a photo to compare yours to. You can Google the author's name and see if fans have posted a facsimile anywhere.

And you can peruse the several websites that perform the public service of cataloging and displaying different authors' signatures—check out such pages as those provided by Purple House Press (www.purplehouse-press.com/sig.htm), My Book House (home.earthlink.net/~criswell/authors/agraphs.htm), and Fadedgiant www.fadedgiant.net/html/signatures_quotes.htm).

If you have time, you can take the step of tracking down in person (or by e-mail or fax) a for-sure authentic signature, from, for instance, a signed limited edition.

The one thing that should inspire no confidence at all in an eBay item's veracity is a seller's offer of a "certificate of authenticity." These certificates are a carryover from the world of sports collectibles, where there seem to be as many obviously phony autographs as real ones. But anyone with a computer—that is, anyone at all—can print out a certificate, write in the appropriate name, and enclose it with a signed book as though it were a real guarantee.

Here's one that accompanied an eBay-purchased copy of the sports biography *Martina*, reading, "This certifies that this book by Martina Navratilova has been hand signed and is authentic." The fact that the book is *about* Navratilova, not *by* her, doesn't help convince me that the scribble is genuine—or that the guy who typed up the certificate knows or cares one way or the other.

### They Just *Look* Like Autographs
Forgeries are hardly the only signed books for sale out there that aren't legit—some signed books aren't really

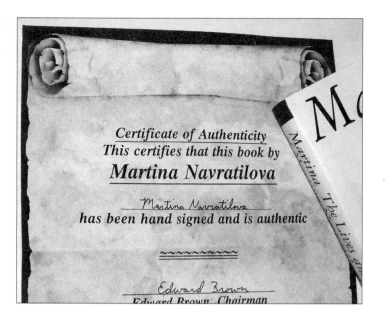

Certificate of Authenticity
This certifies that this book by
**Martina Navratilova**

*Martina Navratilova*

**has been hand signed and is authentic**

~~~~~~~~~~~~

*Edward Brown*
Edward Brown, Chairman

**"Certificate of Authenticity."** In this case, worth no more than the paper it's printed on.

signed at all. An awful lot of volumes carry facsimile autographs on title pages, at the end of introductions and dedications, on covers, and under photos. Most are obviously printed; a few of them you'd *swear* were real.

A good rule of thumb is to see whether *it makes sense* for the author's name to be printed there. If the author's name appears just once on a title page, it's more than likely printed, however real it looks. If it appears under an author photo opposite the title page, and it's the only identification of the person depicted, it's almost certainly printed—even when what's written is a dated inscription, not just an autograph.

Some books show up frequently online as being "signed" that obviously aren't, and you'll soon learn which. To be fair, it's often really hard to determine whether a black-ink signature is real or printed—though in my experience, almost every time that a seller confesses to not being able to tell, the signature is indeed printed. Among the most common: Daphne du Maurier's *Jamaica Inn*, Michael Jackson's *Moonwalk*, Ulysses S. Grant's posthumous *Personal Memoirs*, Aretha Franklin's *From These Roots*, and "autographed editions" by

the likes of Mark Twain and eighteenth-century games guru Edmond Hoyle.

My favorite not-real autographs show up in breathless eBay descriptions: A hardcover missing its dust jacket is said to be autographed on the cover "in gold pen" by an author who pressed hard enough to make an indentation. Take note: No author signs on the cover, much less in gold pen, and no one presses *that* hard.

There are also *autopen* signatures, made by a machine that realistically duplicates an autograph, every signature identical in size and detail. The technology was first widely used by U.S. presidents, who couldn't always be present when important documents required their signatures. Few authors are known to use autopen machines; they're much more common in the sports-collectibles world, where star athletes field hundreds of autograph requests by mail. You'll quickly come to recognize the books that appear for sale most frequently with autopen signatures—among them, Richard Nixon's *Six Crises*, Hillary Clinton's *It Takes a Village*, Bo Jackson's *Bo Knows Bo*, and Michael Crichton's *Jurassic Park*. In all these cases, it's best to hold out for an inscribed copy—that way, you *know* it's really been autographed. An autopen

**They Just *Look* Like Autographs** *(above left).* A signature under a photo on a left-hand page, as in this 1863 Wendell Phillips volume, is probably printed rather than authentically autographed.

**Common Mistake** *(above right).* If the author's name appears just once on the title page, it's probably printed.

**Embarrassing Mistake.** No author signs on the cover, much less in gold pen.

copy is worth more than an unadorned one but a fraction of a genuine signed copy.

*Secretarial* signatures aren't all that common among authors. Perhaps the most frequently seen is that of Martin Luther King Jr., who spent most of his life traveling, leaving staffers to field autograph requests. King's genuine signature is cramped, clumsy, and rare; his secretary's rendition is graceful and flowing. ◼

# 4

# RESOURCE GUIDE

## Online Resources

The Internet offers a breathtaking array of sites that cover every aspect of book collecting, from recommendations of favorite titles to hard-earned warnings of counterfeit books to news of high-level sales at auction to down-and-dirty tips on what's hot and what's not. Among the most useful for beginners are those that collect photos and research on particular genres and eras, such as 1950s pulp fiction or 1920s children's series—they offer ideas and directions to turn, as well as displaying the inspirational passion that drives real enthusiasts.

Collectors start new sites all the time, so it's worth searching the Net periodically for what's fresh. Most sites include a page of links as well, leading you to other vistas.

Some sites worth checking out:

**AddALL:** used.addall.com
**Advanced Book Exchange:** abebooks.com
**Alibris:** www.alibris.com
**Barry R. Levin Science Fiction & Fantasy Literature:** www.raresf.com
**Bauman Rare Books:** www.baumanrarebooks.com
**Bibliomania:** bibliomania.net
**Bibliophile:** www.bibliophile.net
**Book Clubs Directory:** bookclubdeals.com
**Bookfinder:** www.bookfinder.com
**Book Lovers:** www.xs4all.nl/~pwessel
**BookSpot:** www.bookspot.com
**Collecting Books and Magazines:** www.penrithcity.nsw.gov.au/usrpages/Collect/welcome.htm
**Mike Berro's archived FAQs of the rec.collecting.books newsgroup:** www.massmedia.com/~mikeb/rcb
**Fadedgiant:** www.fadedgiant.net
**Online Bookselling Resource Center:** onlinebookselling.net
**Page One Literary Newsletter Web Site Writer's Resources:** pageonelit.com/links.html
**TomFolio:** www.tomfolio.com
**Steve Trussel's compilation of information and links:** www.trussel.com/books.htm
**WantedBooks.com:** www.wantedbooks.com

## Books on Books

It's impossible, of course, to measure bibliophiles' passion against that of other collectors, but it's at least some indication that book lovers are compelled to tell others of their passion. Needless to say, there are no books called *A Life With Coins* or *A Shelf of Old Stamps* or *The Companionship of Depression Glass* or *Among My Franklin Mint Collectible Elvis Plates*.

"There are more books about books than about any other subject," wrote French essayist Michel Eyquem de Montaigne back in the sixteenth century, and in the last five hundred years, the "Books on Books" shelf has widened considerably. Book collectors have produced thousands of volumes about their passion, ranging from dealers' slim monographs published for a handful of top customers to Nicholas Basbanes' chunky memoirs and chronicles. For novice collectors, publishers have offered primers—not entirely unlike this one—for well over a century.

Authors fill book after book with reminiscences of dimly lit bookstores, of tense auctions, of encounters with reclusive authors, of pilgrimages to libraries, of poring over treasures. Most are charmingly told, and always literate, and widen the reader's horizons to new methods of collecting, fresh locations, intriguing sources. The authors' excitement is contagious. But the books may test your patience and tolerance—not in the sense that the essays and anecdotes grow tedious but, rather, that they are about books *that you don't own*. After all, collecting is about more than appreciating pretty books—that's what libraries' special-collection rooms are for. It's because you want to *possess* the books. So how many pages can you read about rival collectors crowing over their once-in-a-lifetime finds? It's up to you.

Every bibliophile has his own favorite books about books; a comprehensive list would run many pages. I've listed a relative handful of representative and favorite titles.

Once you select a specialty, you can turn to specific volumes that'll help show you what's out there to be collected and hint at what's worth going for. Just one example: If you're interested in cookbooks, you'll want to check out Mary Barile's *Cookbooks Worth Collecting*, Linda J. Dickinson's *Price Guide to Cookbooks and Recipe Leaflets*, and Bob Allen's *A Guide to Collecting Cookbooks: A History of People, Companies and Cooking*.

## On Collecting

Allen and Patricia Ahearn, *Book Collecting 2000: A Comprehensive Guide* (Putnam, 2000)—An indispensable, readable introduction and reference work from the collecting world's reigning authorities. Some 335 pages—almost two-thirds of the book—consists of approximate retail values for authors' first books in 1986, 1995, and 2000. It's both surprisingly entertaining and extraordinarily useful as a reference on debut books.

Allen and Patricia Ahearn, *Collected Books: The Guide to Values, 2002 Edition* (Putnam, 2002)—At $75 and 788 pages, this is an intimidating volume to buy, but it's something you'll want on your shelf after a while in the hobby. Composed almost entirely of listings of important books and their approximate values. As with the Ahearns' *Book Collecting*—and with every other book that preserves current price listings between hard covers—values for comparatively recent books are only vaguely accurate.

Nicholas A. Basbanes, *Among the Gently Mad: Perspectives and Strategies for the Book-Hunter in the 21st Century* (Holt, 2002)—A terrific book for the advanced beginner, skipping over the nuts-and-bolts how-to-tell-a-first-edition stuff for overall philosophy and strategy. As the many Basbanes quotes throughout this book attest, he's a wonderfully lucid book-hunting companion.

Nicholas A. Basbanes, *A Gentle Madness: Bibliophiles, Bibliomanes, and the Eternal Passion for Books* (Holt, 1995)—An attractive, hefty volume, this is the definitive history of book collecting in America, with plenty of personality and fun side trips. Not to be missed.

Nicholas A. Basbanes, *Patience & Fortitude: A Roving Chronicle of Book People, Book Places, and Book Culture* (HarperCollins, 2001)—Further excursions into the historical past of bibliophilia—and into the present. Basbanes takes the reader inside dank university libraries, well-traveled bookshops, and magnificent personal collections, all with great insight and enthusiasm.

John Hill Burton, *The Book-Hunter* (Sheldon, 1863)—An all-time classic, still worth reading to learn what collectors of the time emphasized—fine bindings, evidently—and to marvel that a book written nearly a century and a half ago contains so many still-current observations about condition, buying and selling, and the reading and shopping habits of bibliophiles.

John Carter, *ABC for Book Collectors* (Oak Knoll, 2000)—Carter died in 1975, but he remains perhaps the most frequently quoted authority on collecting. *ABC*, consisting of several hundred alphabetical entries—definitions, commentary, and essays—is his best-known title. Nicolas Barker, editor of *The Book Collector*, has revised and updated *ABC*, originally published in 1952, through seven editions.

John Carter, *Taste & Technique in Book Collecting* (Private Libraries Association, 1970)—Serious collectors will find this volume, originally published in 1948, worth tracking down. Carter's observations are laden with wisdom and aphoristic wit that still ring true today.

Ian C. Ellis, *Book Finds: How to Find, Buy and Sell Used and Rare Books* (Perigee, 2001)—A cleanly written, commonsense introduction to collecting, delving into details that most guides overlook. The book's special feature, a list of one-thousand-plus "Most Collectible" books and authors, is interesting but not as useful as Ellis intends it to be.

W. Carew Hazlitt, *The Book Collector: A General Survey of the Pursuit and of Those Who Have Engaged in It at Home and Abroad from the Earliest Period to the Present Time* (John Grant, 1904)—As is obvious from my many quotes from this book, one of my favorite old volumes on bibliophilia, mixing still-applicable wisdom with amusingly dated observations.

Katharine Kyes Leab, *American Book Prices Current* (Bancroft-Parkman)—Produced annually on CD-ROM as well as in book form, *ABPC* is essential for the reference shelf of any bookstore that sells a lot of high-end volumes. It lists more than 750,000 records of in-person (though not online) auction sales since 1975, which is a far more accurate indication of a book's value than what dealers are asking for comparable copies. Unfortunately, *ABPC* starts at $1,680, likely a bit out of your price range. Oh well.

Bill McBride, *Book Collecting for Fun & Profit* (McBride, 2002)—Well-written and extremely concise introduction to the hobby, but this ninety-four-page pamphlet is hard to recommend to anyone already involved in the hobby—$12.95 just seems like a lot for something that weighs but two ounces, and its green paper covers don't contain much material you can't find elsewhere.

Bill McBride, *A Pocket Guide to the Identification of First Editions* (McBride, 2000)—Another self-published pamphlet, one that's far more useful than *Book Collecting*, if not particularly readable in a prose sense. In this case, the book's tiny size works to advantage, since you can tuck it in a purse or pocket. Short of the Zempel-Verkler book listed below, the best single-volume first-edition reference available.

Bill McBride, *Points of Issue: A Compendium of Points of Issue of Books of the 19th and 20th Centuries* (McBride, 1996)—McBride has compiled and packed so much information into these small pages that *Points of Issue* is a standard reference for many dealers. Note, though, that the kind of books for which points of issue are important are seldom those for which you have to make an impulsive decision.

Robert A. Wilson, *Modern Book Collecting* (Knopf, 1980)—Solid advice for those interested in collecting modern first editions. Wilson is authoritative, lucid, and firm, though he wastes little space conveying the hobby's magic and mystery—perhaps he assumes that the reader is already convinced.

Stephen Windwalker, *Buying Books Online: Finding Bargains and Saving Money at Booksense Stores, Amazon's Marketplace, and Other Online Sites* (Harvard Perspectives, 2002)—This self-published softcover is somewhat less useful than its companion book but still worth a read. Windwalker looks at new as well as used books, offering advice about feedback etiquette and using a variety of sites, as well as warnings about shipping costs and misleading descriptions.

Stephen Windwalker, *Selling Used Books Online: The Complete Guide to Bookselling at Amazon's Marketplace and Other Online Sites* (Harvard Perspectives, 2002)— The companion to *Buying Books Online* is full of useful details and tips, particularly for readers interested in beginning part-time businesses. Windwalker focuses so closely on Amazon.com's system, though, that anyone not set up to sell on that site will feel alienated—not to mention that, if Amazon should alter its system soon (always a likely possibility), chunks of the book will be instantly obsolete.

John T. Winterich and David A. Randall, *A Primer of Book Collecting* (Crown, 1966)—Originally published in 1926 and revised in 1935, 1946, and 1966, this remains valuable for its advice about specialization and tips on collecting. Of course, the values it cites are long out of date, but that's OK.

Edward N. Zempel and Linda A. Verkler, *First Editions: A Guide to Identification* (Spoon River, 2001)—A comprehensive, periodically updated, painstakingly compiled reference guide—quoting publishers' edition-identification policies through the years—that contains far more information that you'll likely need, unless you're going into the antiquarian business.

## On Books

Russell Ash and Brian Lake, *Bizarre Books* (Pavilion, 1998)—A marvelous little bathroom-reading paperback cataloging hundreds of the oddest and most obscure volumes ever published.

Nicholas A. Basbanes, *A Splendor of Letters: The Permanence of Books in an Impermanent World* (HarperCollins, 2003)—The latest volume from the marvelous Basbanes, about books' role in societies around the world and their future in an electronic age.

Lionel Casson, *Libraries in the Ancient World* (Yale, 2001)—Concise, authoritative, and entertaining history of official book-accumulating before and after Alexandria.

Richard W. Clement, *The Book in America* (Fulcrum, 1996)—A vigorous overview of U.S. publishing, enlivened by magnificent photos and illustrations.

Estelle Ellis, Caroline Seebohm, and Christopher Simon Sykes, *At Home With Books: How Booklovers Live With and Care for Their Libraries* (Carol Southern, 1995)—Spectacular photographs of libraries and their owners, in a lovely oversize volume that no bibliophile's coffee table should be missing.

Jason Epstein, *Book Business: Publishing Past, Present, and Future* (Norton, 2001)—Brisk, cheerfully personal overview of publishing, from one of the great industry figures.

Anne Fadiman, *Ex Libris: Confessions of a Common Reader* (Farrar, Straus and Giroux, 1998)—A delightful compilation of essays about books and reading.

Lawrence and Nancy Goldstone, *Used and Rare: Travels in the Book World* (St. Martin's, 1997), *Slightly Chipped:*

*Footnotes in Booklore* (St. Martin's, 1999), and *Warmly Inscribed: The New England Forger and Other Book Tales* (St. Martin's, 2001)—Charming though digressive musings about book-hunting. Your fondness for the Goldstones may depend on how much you enjoy reading about other collectors' successful browsing.

Holbrook Jackson, *The Anatomy of Bibliomania* (Farrar, Straus, 1950)—Originally published in 1931, this weighty classic is stuffed with purplish, learned prose about every aspect of loving books, with regard to both reading and collecting. Too dense to skim lightly but immensely rewarding.

Rob Kaplan and Harold Rabinowitz, *Speaking of Books: The Best Things Ever Said About Books and Book Collecting* (Crown, 2001)—A cheery compilation of aphorisms and testimonials about the love of books. More ideal as a gift for a bibliophile than as an essential entry on your own shelf.

Michael Korda, *Making the List: A Cultural History of the American Bestseller 1900–1999* (Barnes & Noble, 2001)— A fascinating catalog of annual best-seller lists from each year of the last century. Korda's introductions, one for each decade, are genial if a bit skimpy. Most valuable are his lamentations at the utter predictability of recent years' best-sellers: A dozen popular mediocrities dominate the list and leave little room for fresh voices.

Henry Petroski, *The Book on the Bookshelf* (Knopf, 1999)—Frequently illuminating (though with more detail and background than many readers will want) musings on the history of books and the shelves that hold them.

Tom Raabe, *Biblioholism: The Literary Addiction* (Fulcrum, 2001)—A half-serious parody of self-help books that is often as true as it is amusing. Hardly necessary but a lot of fun.

Frederic Raphael and Kenneth McLeish, *The List of Books* (Harmony, 1981)—Contentious but surprisingly useful guide to creating a ideal home library of three thousand titles, including representative and standard works in every subject area from architecture to geography to mythology to crime thrillers.

André Schiffrin, *The Business of Books* (Verso, 2000)—Blending history and memoir, Schiffrin describes how the increasing corporatization of publishing led him to quit his longtime post as managing director of Pantheon and found an independent publishing house. Eloquent, heartfelt, and ultimately depressing about the future of bookmaking and -selling.

John Tebbel, *Between Covers: The Rise and Transformation of Book Publishing in America* (Oxford, 1987)—At 514 pages, Tebbel's condensation of his definitive four-volume *A History of Book Publishing in the United States* is marvelously readable and tremendously informative. What's amazing is that the full-blown, 3,000-odd-page *History* (check your local college library) is itself a fun read and fleshes out the stories and analysis in *Between Covers*. Essential for any bibliophile.

## Magazines
*The Book Collector*: www.thebookcollector.co.uk
*The Bookseller*: www.thebookseller.com
*Firsts: The Book Collector's Magazine*: www.firsts.com
*ForeWord Magazine*: www.forewordmagazine.com
*Pages: The Magazine for People Who Love Books*:
www.ireadpages.com
*Publishers Weekly*: www.publishersweekly.com
*Publishing News*: www.publishingnews.co.uk
*The Readerville Journal*: www.readerville.com

## Museums, Associations, and Organizations
American Booksellers Association: www.bookweb.org
Antiquarian Booksellers Association of America: abaa.org
Fellowship of American Bibliophilic Societies:
www.fabsbooks.org
Grolier Club: www.grolierclub.org
Huntington Library: www.huntington.org
International League of Antiquarian Booksellers:
www.ilab-lila.com
Library of Congress: www.loc.gov
New York Public Library: www.nypl.org

## Conventions and Sales
Antiquarian Book Fairs: www.bookfairs.com
BookExpo America: www.bookexpoamerica.com
Book Sale Finder: www.booksalefinder.com
California International Antiquarian Book Fair:
californiabookfair.com
Edinburgh International Book Festival: www.edbookfest.co.uk

**Frankfurt Book Fair:** www.frankfurt-book-fair.com
**The *Guardian* Hay Festival:** www.hayfestival.com
**London Book Fair:** www.lbf-virtual.com
**New York Is Book Country:** www.nyisbookcountry.com
**Rare Book School:** www.virginia.edu/old/books
**Used and Antiquarian Book Fairs:**
www.bookhunterpress.com/index.cgi/bkfairs.html

## Supplies

All these sites offer a variety of materials and accessories
to help preserve and repair books—in particular, dust-
jacket protectors. Different collectors and dealers have
different preferences, beginning with Brodart and Gaylord. Check out all of them. If you like the way books that
come from a certain used bookseller look and feel, note
which company manufactured the DJ protectors and try
ordering from that company. Also worth checking out is
"A Simple Book Repair Manual," published by the Dart-
mouth College Library: www.dartmouth.edu/~preserve/
repair/repairindex.htm. And take note of a terrific site on
book conservation—including aids to help you locate a
bookbinder or conservator in your area—at palimpsest.
stanford.edu.

**Brodart:** www.brodart.com
**Bill Cole Enterprises:** bcemylar.com
**Demco:** www.demco.com
**Gaylord:** www.gaylord.com
**Hollinger:** www.genealogicalstorageproducts.com
**Metal Edge:** www.metaledgeinc.com
**University Products:** www.universityproducts.com
**Vernon Library Supplies:** www.vernlib.com

## Cataloging Software

**BookCAT:** www.fnprg.com/bookcat/bookcat.html
**Book Collector:** www.collectorz.com/book
**Book Collector Pro:**
www.radleyhouse.com/BookCollectorPro.htm
**Book 'em:** oldlib.com/bookem
**BookHound:** www.bookhound.net
**Book Librarian Plus:**
www.turbosysco.com/turbosys/booklib95sin.html
**Book Organizer:** www.primasoft.com/32org/32bko.htm
**BookTrakker:** booktrakker.com
**Home Library XP:** www.datavillage.com/homelibraryxp.htm
**My Book Collection:** www.mybookcollection.com
**Organize! Your Collection:**
www.homecraft.com/OYC/BOOKS/index.html

**QBook:** www.qbbooks.com/qbook.htm
**QCollector:** www.qbbooks.com/qcollect.htm
**SmartTracker Books:** www.wintools.com/stbooks/index.htm

## Shops

The country's biggest secondhand bookshops are well-known. Among them: Book Baron (Anaheim, California), Book Barn (Niantic, Connecticut), Brattle Book Shop (Boston), John K. King Used and Rare Books (Detroit), Moe's (Berkeley), Powell's (Portland, Oregon), Second Story (Washington, D.C.), The Strand (New York), and Wonder Book (Frederick, Maryland). Any are certainly worth a stop if you're anywhere near the neighborhood; in the case of Booked Up, novelist Larry McMurtry's middle-of-nowhere empire, the store is just about the only reason to visit Archer City, Texas.

For smaller stores—which may still be pretty huge—search the usual: Google in case local bibliophiles have compiled information and tips, and yellow-pages listings. There's also David and Susan Siegel's series of *Used Book Lover's Guides*, regional references essential for those who seek out bookstores wherever they vacation. The softcover books are updated annually, and in 2000 the Siegels made their entire database available online by subscription. It's still a good idea, of course, to phone ahead to make sure a particular store is still operating a walk-in business. ◼

# 5

# THE INSTANT EXPERT QUIZ

**1.** If a book's copyright page states "First Edition," is it unquestionably a first edition?

**2.** If a book's copyright page contains the letter sequence C D E, what printing is it?

**3.** What do a book's *points* help a collector determine?

**4.** Are limited editions always scarcer and more desirable than regular editions of the same book?

**5.** What does a missing price on a book's jacket flap usually indicate?

**6.** When is a British or Canadian first edition worth more than its American counterpart?

**7.** How few copies of a book must exist for it to be considered genuinely rare?

**8.** What are the main advantages to shopping at a bookstore rather than online?

**9.** Can you trust online booksellers to know more than you do about identifying first editions?

**10.** When you're selling online, when is it acceptable to describe a book as *nice* or *mint*?

**11.** Is it *ever* OK to throw away a book?

**12.** What impact does a literary prize have on an author's collectibility?

**13.** In general, do business books have good resale value?

**14.** How much does it matter that a book has its dust jacket?

**15.** Under what circumstances is an ex-library copy worth buying?

**16.** Is it OK to mark your own first editions with an ownership stamp?

**17.** Why do some books have remainder marks?

**18.** Do collectible books always hold their value?

**19.** Did nineteenth-century authors tend to autograph books under their photos?

**20.** What's *foxing*?

## Answers

**1.** Certainly not. It depends on the publisher: Sometimes a "First Edition" note is enough of an indication, but often there's a number sequence or other marker to help determine a first.

**2.** A third printing. Letter sequences traditionally begin with A, but even in the cases when they begin with B, a C as the first letter indicates a third printing.

**3.** Which printing or state a book is, that can't be determined by the usual first-edition indicators. Publishers alter many books partway through their printings, leaving clues, such as which blurbs are featured on the DJ or the number of introductory blank pages. For collectors, the earliest copies are, of course, more valuable, so they strive to catalog which version came first.

**4.** Surprisingly, no. Publishers always intend limited editions to be more valuable, but years after a book's publication, the regular first edition may actually be harder to find, since no one throws away limited editions of *anything*. There's also the issue of whether "manufactured rarities" *deserve* to be more valuable.

**5.** Except for some university-press titles, a price-free DJ flap almost always means that a book is a book-club edition—to be avoided at any cost!

**6.** When an author is from Britain or Canada, a first published in his home country is usually worth more than one published simultaneously here. The practice of privileging a writer's home-country titles is called "following the flag."

**7.** Technically, a *rare* book is one of which only a literal handful of copies are known to exist—say, under two dozen. But that's a definition that's unrealistically strict when it comes to book collecting, considering that some books get first printings in the millions.

**8.** At a bookstore, you don't have to worry that something you're buying is the wrong edition, or in worse condition than promised. More than anything, you can browse, meaning that you'll run across titles you weren't looking for and may not have even known existed.

**9.** Absolutely not—the Internet has made it so easy to sell books that thousands of amateurs have put their collections up for sale without necessarily doing their homework. And as you're by now quite aware, there's an awful lot to know!

**10.** *Mint* is an appropriate term to describe the condition of a coin, but never of a book. And *nice* is fine only so long as it comes after a more official description—and so long as you don't mind not being taken seriously.

**11.** With millions of new books entering the world every single year, room must be made, and you shouldn't feel bad about discarding damaged copies of common books. Well, maybe you should feel a little bad, but just a little.

**12.** A major prize always gives that book a boost in value, but there's no rule about whether the rest of the author's work will be carried along—or even whether the prize book's value increase will dissipate altogether in the months following the award ceremony.

**13.** The vast majority of business books have no market value whatsoever—which means that while you shouldn't buy them to resell, you can *collect* them for a song.

**14.** For books published after 1930 or so, the dust jacket is often worth far more than the book itself. So indeed, it matters a lot.

**15.** You should consider buying an ex-library copy only when it's a book that is truly desirable and *very* inexpensive. Keep in mind that an ex-library copy will never be more than a placeholder.

**16.** Ownership stamps are pretty cool, but you should *never* use them to mark anything but pure reading copies. If you absolutely must loan out collectible books, try personalized bookmarks.

**17.** When a printing of a book doesn't sell out, for whatever reason, its publisher is stuck with hundreds or thousands of warehoused copies. To make space, it sells the copies to resellers who mark them as remainders—to distinguish them from full-price copies—and offer them to bookstores to sell at dramatic discounts.

**18.** If only! The history of collecting is full of booms and crashes. The two most recent dips came with the recession of the early 1990s, when the prices of fine art and other expensive collectibles sank, and several years ago, when Internet sales drove down prices of modern first editions.

**19.** It just looks that way at first glance. When there's an author photo in an old book—particularly opposite the title page—and it has a signature underneath, it's almost certainly pre-printed.

**20.** I *knew* you'd ask! *Foxing* is the brownish discoloration that mars the pages of some older books, particularly those made with heavily acidic paper.

# 6

# MARKET TRENDS

These values are for unsigned first editions, first printings, with dust jackets, in NF/NF condition, and represent the low end of what online sellers are offering these books for. That's not to say that they're necessarily good deals at these prices: Those sky-high prices for nonfiction books published in the last few years—for instance, *Seabiscuit*—will almost surely fall in the *next* few. The track record for best-selling nonfiction isn't good.

This is less a guide to the prices of truly valuable items you can find online or at a swanky store than it is a sampling of books you very well might run across at a bookstore or library sale. The important thing is to get a general sense of what's collectible, what's not—and what might be.

I should note that when you're scanning prices from on-line booksellers on, say, Advanced Book Exchange, it's easy to get thrown off by those who price items aston-ishingly high, clearly out of the normal range. I queried one bookseller who consistently prices his books at two to four times the going rate; he replied, "I believe that being the lowest price is not my goal nor the goal of most of my members." Evidently, high pricing is a strat-egy that works for him—a number of book-shoppers are willing to dramatically overpay for the comfort of buying from a familiar seller.

But that's hardly a model for you to follow, and you shouldn't take those high prices too seriously. Just be-cause someone is selling a first edition of Robin Cook's novel *Outbreak*—a $5 book—for $49 doesn't mean it's *worth* $49.

**Mitch Albom**
*Tuesdays with Morrie (1997)*                                     $7–20

**Stephen E. Ambrose**
*Band of Brothers (1992)*                                      $350–450

**Stephen E. Ambrose**
*Undaunted Courage (1996)*                                      $20–30

**Richard Bach**
*Illusions: The Adventures of a Reluctant Messiah (1977)*  $8–20

**Richard Bach**
*Out of My Mind: The Discovery of Saunders-Vixen (1999)*  $3–7

**Dave Barry**
*Dave Barry Turns 40 (1990)*                                      $1–4

**A. Scott Berg**
*Lindbergh (1998)*                                                $4–8

**Allan Bloom**
*The Closing of the American Mind (1987)*                        $10–15

**Richard Blow**
*American Son: A Portrait of John F. Kennedy, Jr. (2002)*  $8–12

**Robert Bly**
*Iron John: A Book About Men (1990)*                              $2–4

**Daniel Boorstin**
*The Discoverers (1983)*                                          $8–12

**Dan Brown**
*Angels and Demons (2000)*                                     $300–400

**Dan Brown**
*The Da Vinci Code (2003)*                                       $30–50

**Bill Bryson**
*A Walk in the Woods (1997)* $6–9

**Barbara Bush**
*Barbara Bush: A Memoir (1994)* $3–6

**Deepak Chopra**
*Ageless Body, Timeless Mind (1993)* $1–3

**Marcia Clark**
*Without a Doubt (1997)* $1–2

**James Clavell**
*Shogun (1975)* $80–100

**James Clavell**
*Noble House (1981)* $4–7

**Michael Cunningham**
*At Home in the World (1990)* $12–15

**Michael Cunningham**
*The Hours (1998)* $50–65

**Clive Cussler**
*Raise the Titanic! (1976)* $30–50

**Clive Cussler**
*Inca Gold (1994)* $3–5

**Rosie Daley**
*In the Kitchen with Rosie: Oprah's Favorite Recipes (1994)* $1–3

**Ellen Degeneres**
*My Point . . . and I Do Have One (1995)* $1–2

**Don DeLillo**
*White Noise (1985)* $40–65

**Don DeLillo**
*Underworld (1997)* $8–10

**Alan Dershowitz**
*Reversal of Fortune: Inside the Von Bulow Case (1986)* $8–12

**Annie Dillard**
*Pilgrim at Tinker Creek (1974)* $20–40

**Annie Dillard**
*The Living (1992)* $2–5

**Dave Eggers**
*A Heartbreaking Work of Staggering Genius (2000)* $25–35

**Janet Evanovich**
*One for the Money (1994)* $150–200

**Janet Evanovich**
*Hot Six (2000)* $7–9

**Thomas Friedman**
*From Beirut to Jerusalem (1989)* $15–20

**Robert Fulghum**
*All I Really Need to Know I Learned in Kindergarten*
*(1988)* $1–3

**Bill Gates**
*The Road Ahead (1995)* $1–2

**Malcolm Gladwell**
*The Tipping Point (2000)* $15–20

**Daniel Jonah Goldhagen**
*Hitler's Willing Executioners (1996)* $10–15

**Doris Kearns Goodwin**
*Wait Till Next Year (1997)* $4–7

**Sue Grafton**
*A Is for Alibi (1982)* $500–800

**Sue Grafton**
*G Is for Gumshoe (1990)* $10–12

**John Grisham**
*The Firm (1991)* $50–70

**John Grisham**
*The Chamber (1994)* $1–2

**Thomas Harris**
*Red Dragon (1981)* $10–15

**Thomas Harris**
*Hannibal (1999)* $1–2

**Stephen W. Hawking**
*A Brief History of Time (1988)* $4–7

**William Least Heat-Moon**
*Blue Highways: A Journey into America (1982)* $12–20

**Joseph Heller**
*Something Happened (1974)* $3–6

**Joseph Heller**
*Closing Time (1994)* $3–5

**Laura Hillenbrand**
*Seabiscuit: An American Legend (2001)* $300–350

**Philip K. Howard**
*The Death of Common Sense (1995)* $4–6

**Arianna Huffington**
*The Fourth Instinct: The Call of the Soul (1994)* $4–5

**John Irving**
*The World According to Garp (1978)* $70–100

**John Irving**
*A Widow for One Year (1998)* $5–8

**Susan Isaacs**
*Shining Through (1988)* $1–2

**Michael Jackson**
*Moonwalk (1988)* $10–15

**Jerry B. Jenkins and Tim Lahaye**
*Left Behind (1995)* $50–70

**Sebastian Junger**
*The Perfect Storm: A True Story of Men Against the Sea*
*(1997)* $15–25

**Garrison Keillor**
*Lake Wobegon Days (1985)* $4–6

**Garrison Keillor**
*Leaving Home: A Collection of Lake Wobegon Stories*
*(1987)* $2–4

**Tracy Kidder**
*The Soul of a New Machine (1981)* $8–15

**Tracy Kidder**
*Among Schoolchildren (1989)* $1–2

**Stephen King**
*The Shining (1977)* $200–250

**Stephen King**
*Cujo (1981)* $10–15

**Stephen King**
*Insomnia (1994)* $4–5

**Norman Mailer**
*The Naked and the Dead (1948)* $200–400

**Norman Mailer**
*The Armies of the Night (1968)* $8–15

**Norman Mailer**
*Oswald's Tale (1995)* $4–7

**Cormac McCarthy**
*All the Pretty Horses (1992)* $100–175

**Cormac McCarthy**
*The Crossing (1994)* $3–6

**Larry McMurtry**
*Lonesome Dove (1985)* $80–120

**James Michener**
*The Source (1965)* $40–60

**James Michener**
*Chesapeake (1978)* $5–8

**Michael Moore**
*Downsize This! (1996)* $8–12

**John Naisbitt**
*Megatrends: Ten New Directions Transforming Our Lives*
*(1982)* $1–3

**John Naisbitt and Patricia Auburdene**
*Megatrends 2000 (2000)* $1–3

**Nicholas Negroponte**
*Being Digital (1995)* $3–5

**Shaquille O'Neal**
*Shaq Attack! (1993)* $3–6

**Susan Orlean**
*The Orchid Thief (1998)* $15–25

**Chuck Palahniuk**
*Fight Club (1996)* $150–180

**Robert M. Pirsig**
*Zen and the Art of Motorcycle Maintenance (1974)* $100–120

**Robert M. Pirsig**
*Lila: An Inquiry into Morals (1991)* $3–5

**Colin Powell**
*My American Journey: An Autobiography (1995)* $5–7

**Susan Powter**
*Stop the Insanity! (1993)* $1–2

**Howard Rheingold**
*Virtual Reality: Exploring the Brave New Technologies (1991)* $3–6

**Anne Rice**
*Interview With the Vampire (1976)* $350–400

**Anne Rice**
*Memnoch the Devil (1995)* $4–5

**Tom Robbins**
*Still Life with Woodpecker (1980)* $100–150

**Tom Robbins**
*Skinny Legs & All (1990)* $5–8

**Nora Roberts**
*Hidden Riches (1994)* $10–15

**Nora Roberts**
*Carolina Moon (2000)* $2–3

**Dennis Rodman**
*Bad as I Wanna Be (1996)* $3–6

**J.K. Rowling**
*Harry Potter and the Sorcerer's Stone (1998)* $1,500

**J.K. Rowling**
*Harry Potter and the Goblet of Fire (2000)* $17–25

**Laura Schlessinger**
*How Could You Do That? (1996)* $1–2

**Eric Schlosser**
*Fast Food Nation (2001)* $80–100

**Robert Schuller**
*Tough Times Never Last, but Tough People Do! (1983)*   $4–8

**Alice Sebold**
*Lucky (1999)*   $50–80

**Alice Sebold**
*The Lovely Bones (2002)*   $15–25

**Monica Seles**
*Monica: From Fear to Victory (1996)*   $2–5

**George Stephanopoulos**
*All Too Human: A Political Education (1999)*   $2–5

**Howard Stern**
*Private Parts (1993)*   $2–5

**Amy Tan**
*The Joy Luck Club (1989)*   $75–100

**Amy Tan**
*The Hundred Secret Senses (1995)*   $2–4

**Deborah Tannen**
*You Just Don't Understand: Women and Men
in Conversation (1990)*   $1–5

**Margaret Thatcher**
*The Path to Power (1995)*   $5–8

**John Updike**
*Rabbit, Run (1960)*   $500–800

**John Updike**
*Couples (1968)*   $10–13

**John Updike**
*Brazil (1994)*   $4–6

**Kurt Vonnegut**
*Slaughterhouse-Five (1969)*   $500–800

**Kurt Vonnegut**
*Jailbird (1979)*   $5–10

**David Foster Wallace**
*Infinite Jest (1996)*   $30–45

**John Walsh**
*Tears of Rage (1997)*   $4–6

# Glossary

### Advance Reading Copy

A copy, usually softcover, that a publisher prints to promote a forthcoming book. They're distributed to the people who have the power to make a book a bestseller—among them, critics and bookstore owners. Often used synonymously with *galley* and *proof*.

### Antiquarian

When applied to a particular book, it usually connotes something from the nineteenth century or earlier—that is, more than a hundred years old. An *antiquarian bookstore* is one that specializes in old books and, typically, caters to serious collectors and prices books on the high side. Don't drop into a shop with "Antiquarian" over the door and hope for a dollar bin filled with treasures.

### As Issued

The original state. You'll see this most commonly in descriptions of modern books that are issued with slipcases or without dust jackets: "No DJ, as issued."

### Association Copy

A copy of a book that belonged to someone associated with the author. Most typically, a copy inscribed by the author to a friend or relative; most desirably, one inscribed to a famous friend. Association copies (in contrast to those inscribed to someone anonymous) are by their nature unique; when both author and dedicatee are famous, the item can be worth substantially more than a simple autographed book. Technically, a book that *belonged* to someone noteworthy (evidenced by a bookplate or annotations) is an association copy, though one less meaningful, since there's no direct connection between author and owner.

### Autopen

A machine that duplicates an author's signature, usually used only by *very* public figures—for instance, U.S. presidents—and on certain books.

### Backlist

Everything an author published before the one on the New Releases shelf; technically, all those books that are still in print.

### Bibliophile

Simply, someone who loves books. Someone who loves books out of all proportion to reality is a *bibliomaniac*; someone who can't stop buying books is a *biblioholic*. Be prepared for those close to you to apply the latter two terms freely as you get deeper into the hobby.

### Blind Stamp

Blind stamping is the process that embosses a design or image in a book cover without color or gilding. A book-club-edition mark is called a blind stamp, though the process is technically called *debossing*.

### Blurb

A quote on a dust jacket or (in a paperback) first couple of pages extolling the virtues of the book you're holding. Much less useful than you'd think in determining whether a book is worth a) reading or b) collecting. The term was coined in 1907 by humorist Gelett Burgess, who sketched a blonde—dubbed "Miss Blinda Blurb"—as cover art for a dust jacket.

### Book-club Edition

A copy published specifically by or for a book club. Often more cheaply made and *always* less collectible than the regular trade edition.

### Bookplate

A sticker or pasted-in sheet denoting ownership of a book, usually on the endpaper. Bookplates range widely in size and design, from plain and anonymous "From the Library of" stickers to elaborate, full-blown personal designs. A famous person's bookplate—particularly with a signature—carries value in and of itself. Indeed, some people collect bookplates irrespective of the books themselves.

### Bound Galleys

Technically, a book manuscript typeset before final for-matting for the purposes of scanning for typographical errors. In practice, often used synonymously with *proof*, *advanced reading copy*, and plain old *galleys*.

### Broadside

Something printed on one side of an oversize sheet of paper. In the context of book collecting, usually refers to a poem or short story printed on heavy paper stock, in a limited quantity by a small publisher.

**Bumped**
When a corner of a book is blunted or slightly bent from being, well, bumped.

**Chapbook**
A small-format pamphlet.

**Closed Tear**
A tear to, usually, the dust jacket in which there's no paper loss—that is, if you neatly closed the tear, put the DJ in a plastic cover, and stepped back a few feet, you wouldn't see anything wrong.

**Colophon**
A publisher's ornamental insignia, typically appearing on the title page. The original though now less-used meaning: a page at the back of the book offering information on edition and printing.

**Cut Signature**
An autograph or inscription that's been sliced from some document (e.g., a letter) and either laid in or tipped in to a book.

**Device**
Usually refers to a publisher's identifying mark: an owl for Henry Holt, a house for Random House, a telescope-gazing man riding a dolphin for Houghton Mifflin, and so on.

**Dust Jacket, Dustwrapper**
The paper covering a hardcover book's boards.

**Edition**
When a book is revised or reformatted, it's called a new edition. A single edition can go through any number of printings.

**Endpapers**
The first and last leaves of a book, connecting the front and back boards to the text itself. Sometimes plain, sometimes decorated.

**Ephemera**
From the word *ephemeral*, meaning something not intended to last. In this context, it refers to newspaper

clippings, handbills, press releases, magazines, or other paper items that weren't meant to be saved.

### Errata Slip
Typically, a slip of paper inserted into a book to explain or apologize for mistakes in the text. A publisher will do this when an error arises that's too serious to let slide (e.g., two pages being transposed, as with the first printing of Jonathan Franzen's *The Corrections*) but that's not serious enough to take the drastic and expensive measure of yanking the book off store shelves and reprinting it.

### Ex-library
A book that's been discarded by a library—whether public, school, or private circulating—and bears any indication of its origin: stamps, labels, glued-down dust jacket, rebinding, card pocket.

### Ex Libris
From someone's personal library, as evidenced by an ownership bookplate, signature, or blind stamp. You see this notation in listings usually only when the owner is famous; otherwise it's simply "prior owner signature" or "bookplate."

### First Edition
Literally, the first edition of a book, before it's revised. But in common parlance, *first edition* means *first edition, first printing*.

### First Thus
Not the *true first edition*, but the first printing of any later edition—say, a trade paperback edition, a new translation, or an illustrated version.

### First Trade Edition
The first edition available to the public; usually used after a limited edition.

### Flatsigned
A term characterizing books plainly autographed without inscription. Has begun to slip into the general book-collecting lexicon despite there being nothing wrong with the word *autographed*.

## Foxing

The brownish discoloration of a book's pages. Frequently found in older books whose paper contains acid: The acid makes the paper more porous and therefore more susceptible to staining from dust, moisture, or fingerprints. Iron particles and fungus cause slightly different types of foxing.

## Front Free Endpaper

The right side of the *endpaper*—the first blank right-hand page when you open a book. Often abbreviated FFEP or FEP. Some authors—particularly those in a hurry—sign books on this page, since it requires no flipping and has plenty of space.

## Front Matter

Everything before the first page of text: front free end flap, half title page, title page, table of contents, introduction, acknowledgments, and any extra blank or printed pages.

## GGA

Stands for "good girl art"; used to describe pulp paperbacks from the 1950s and 1960s that are particularly risqué. Many mystery novels, sci-fi stories, and true-crime sagas feature scantily clad damsels in distress—from today's perspective, always good for a snicker (or shudder).

## Half Title

The page before the title page, usually bearing only the book's title. Some authors prefer to sign books on this page, since there's more blank space.

## Hand Signed

Autographed in person rather than by a secretary or autopen machine. Since that covers just about everything, a fairly redundant term.

## High Spots

Books that are desirable collectibles apart from being a component of a focused collection—e.g., first editions of Hemingway, Faulkner, Poe, Shakespeare, etc.

### Hinge
Where the front and back covers meet the spine. Technically, *hinge* refers to the internal juncture; *joint* is the exterior juncture. For obvious reasons, this is where older books are most vulnerable. See *Starting*.

### Holograph
A classy way of saying that an item—say, a letter or manuscript—is in the author's handwriting.

### Hypermodern
A first edition published after 1990 or so, particularly one produced in mass quantities.

### Imprint
In the publishing industry, refers to the company division responsible for publishing a given book. For instance, House of Collectibles is an imprint of Random House Information Group, which is itself a division of Random House.

### Inscribed
Autographed, plus additional words—anything from "Best wishes" to a full-page inscription.

### ISBN
Short for International Standard Book Number, an ISBN is a 10-digit number that identifies books and similar products. A book's ISBN is unique and changes with each new edition.

### Laid In
Used to describe an unattached bookplate or ephemera (for instance, a press release about the book) that accompanies the book and has been placed inside the front cover. See *Tipped In*.

### Later Printing
Within an edition, every printing after the first one. Sometimes, publishers make it easy to determine which printing a book is; other times, all that's apparent is that a book is *not* a first. Hence, *later printing*. Book-club editions don't qualify.

### Limited Edition
An edition published in a finite quantity and, typically, to a limited audience. Encompasses both ten-copy editions

signed in the author's blood and the 350,000-copy special edition of *Harry Potter and the Order of the Phoenix*.

**Marbled**
When the publisher has decorated the edges of a book with swirls of colors vaguely resembling marble.

**Marrying**
Bringing together a book and dust jacket that originally had different partners. *Marrying* lets you create a complete copy out of two incomplete ones, which is great, but if the switch is evident—and surprisingly often, it is—collectors frown upon it.

**Mint**
A word that should never be used to describe a book's condition, since books—unlike coins—are not in fact *minted*. There's nothing wrong with *as new*, which is what is meant.

**Modern**
For decades, collectors used *modern* to describe any book that wasn't *antiquarian*—that is, a book from the twentieth century. But what does it mean now? A good bet: anything dated 1920 to 1990. For after 1990, use *hypermodern*.

**No Date**
When a book (usually an antiquarian book) bears no date: on the title page, half title page . . . anywhere. Sometimes you have to estimate a book's age from clues: the way the binding looks, the ads in back, the title-page typeface.

**No Place**
A book that lists no publisher or place of publishing is likely self-published, though there are exceptions, of course.

**A Note on the Type**
A statement on a page at the back of a book that describes the typeface used. Alfred A. Knopf introduced the practice in 1926 to highlight the care with which his imprint's books were produced.

**Octavo**
A book that's approximately six by nine inches. There's a whole list of archaic printer's terms describing book

sizes and makeup, none of which you really need to know. The term *octavo* comes from the book's being printed on sheets that are folded to make eight leaves, or sixteen pages.

### Out of Print
When a publisher decides that a book's shelf life is over—that no new demand is likely to arise—it may take the book *out of print* and sell off any leftover copies to remainder dealers. This doesn't preclude the publisher, or a different one, bringing the book back into print at a later date, but it's a declaration that for the time being, no new copies will be printed.

### Paperback
A volume with flexible covers rather than stiff boards.

### Paperback Original
A book whose first publication is as a paperback rather than a hardcover. Abbreviated PBO. Introduced in 1930, when Simon & Schuster published six fiction titles as PBOs, and widely seen in the mid-1980s when Vintage brought out dozens of debut novels. Far more common today in England than in the States.

### Pastedown
The left side of the *endpaper*—that is, the paper lining of the inside of the front cover.

### Pirated Edition
A copy printed without the permission (or even knowledge) of the real publisher or author. In a few cases, a book has had copyright or legal problems preventing regular publication, and enterprising rogues have rushed out unauthorized editions. More commonly, once in a while you might run across an edition of, say, a 1970s Philip Roth novel that looks *almost* like the real thing but is printed on cheaper paper and has the feel of a photocopy—and isn't a BCE. When you discover the Chinese characters on the title page, the mystery is solved. These pirated editions aren't particularly collectible.

### Placeholder Copy
A book—a later printing or substandard-condition copy—that you keep until you can locate, or afford, a better copy. It's best to skip this stage altogether: Why waste

the money and space on something you're already plot-
ting to discard?

**Plate**
A page of illustration, typically on heavy or glossy stock,
that's tipped or bound into a book.

**Pocketbooks**
Small-format softcovers, also known as *mass-market paperbacks*. Introduced in 1939 by reprint publisher Robert
Fair de Graff after a series of price wars that wreaked
havoc on sales strategies and book quality. De Graff's
line of pocket-size paperbacks—called, appropriately,
Pocket Books—were an instant success, and other publishers followed suit.

**Points**
The clues used in determining which *printing* or *state* a
book is: the color of the binding, changes in dust-jacket
text—the possibilities are endless, and they differ for
each book that has variations.

**Presentation Copy**
One of the author's personal copies, presented to someone else. Usually but not always autographed, and distinct from a regular inscribed copy.

**Printing**
Each new run of books within a given edition. Synonymous with *impression*.

**Privately Printed**
A book printed, often by the author himself, for private
circulation rather than for sale.

**Provenance**
Proof of a book's history—for instance, a photograph of
an author signing or a reference in a letter that the particular book was owned by a certain person.

**Quarto**
Describes a book that's approximately twelve inches tall.
Like *octavo*, a bookmaking term that's not all that useful.

**Rare**
A used book that's both collectible and somewhat difficult to find. With Internet-expanded availability, older

definitions of scarcity—say, a book that you might run across a couple of times a decade—are no longer particularly relevant.

### Reading Copy
What a seller calls a book that's not really in collectible condition but is nevertheless complete. Alternately, a second copy of a book (often a paperback) that you own for the purpose of reading rather than simply preserving. "If you buy a book with anything in mind other than collecting," writes Ian C. Ellis, "you're buying a reading copy."

### Rebinding
The process of taking apart a book ("disbinding") and putting it together with new, fancy covers. Any book listed as "a good candidate for rebinding" is a poor candidate for buying in the first place.

### Remainder
A book marked as overstock with a dot, stripe, or spray on the top or bottom of the text block.

### Salesman's Dummy
A book—typically from the first couple of decades of the last century—carried door-to-door by a salesman collecting orders for the finished book. A dummy usually contains mostly blank pages.

### Secondhand
A used book that's not collectible enough to qualify as *rare*.

### Shaken
On the verge of coming apart—that is, the text block is coming loose from the binding.

### Slipcase
A cardboard box, typically open on one side, that serves in lieu of a dust jacket, usually for special or limited editions of books. Occasionally, slipcased books have jackets as well.

### Starting
When a book's *hinge* has become noticeably fragile, it is described as *starting*. As Robert A. Wilson writes, "Cataloguers apparently cannot bring themselves to complete

the phrase by saying 'starting to fall apart.'" Starting is usually signified by the endpaper's splitting.

### State
The priority of copies within a particular edition, the first being the most desirable. You'll see descriptions such as "First edition, second state," meaning that something (for instance, the color of the binding) changed during the printing of the first edition. *State* is basically synonymous with *issue*.

### Sunned
What you call a book that's spent time in direct sunlight and has faded and discolored as a result. Most typically, a description will state "Spine sunned." Purple and green covers are most susceptible.

### Tipped In
A page or other paper (e.g., a bookplate or cut signature) that's pasted into the book, as opposed to being bound in or *laid in*.

### Title Page
The first page that lists the author, book title, and publisher. The usual page on which an author autographs a book. Indeed, notes Anne Fadiman in *Ex Libris*, "proper inscription etiquette" demands that *only* a book's author be allowed to write on the title page.

### Trade Paperback
A softcover book that's closer in size to a hardcover than to a mass-market paperback. Introduced in the 1950s by Anchor Books, a Doubleday imprint, the creation of executive Jason Epstein, who later left Doubleday to help Random House develop the Vintage series of trade paperbacks.

### True First Edition
The very first appearance of the book (apart from advance copies), even if only by a day. The term *true first* is overused: Some sellers excitedly apply it to every first edition, no matter how common or clear.

### Uncorrected Proof
An advance copy printed after author revisions but before final formatting. Often used synonymously with *galley* and *advance reading copy*.

### Uncut

Pages that don't line up exactly in the text block and therefore have a handmade feel. Many older books are *uncut*, and a few publishers—most notably Knopf—still use the technique today. *Uncut* is not the same as *unopened*, which refers to a book that has some pages still unseparated.

### Uniform Edition

Also called a *collected edition*. A publisher's reissue of some or all of an author's works, in a fresh and uniform design, generally in trade paperback but occasionally in hardcover. Until recent decades, collected editions typically brought out works by established, deceased authors. Today, a new uniform edition is usually occasioned by popular or critical interest in one of an author's books; unsurprisingly, the new edition often mimics that book's design.

### Unsophisticated

Unrestored in any way: no rebinding, regluing, retouching. Irrespective of condition: An unsophisticated copy may be fine or poor.

### Wartime Editions

Reprints published during World War II in smaller format and with thinner paper due to restrictions on materials usage. These books are always labeled as wartime editions, leaving the impression that the buyer is committing an act of patriotism.

### Wraps

The soft covers on a paperback book, from mass-market paperbacks to trade paperbacks to oversize softcovers.

# INDEX